Risotto Cookbook

Delicious Risotto Recipes in an Easy
Risotto Cookbook

By
BookSumo Press

Published by
http://www.booksumo.com

Table of Contents

Sonoma Orzo Risotto 7

Risotto Mexicana 8

Vegan Dessert Risotto 9

Alleghany Mushroom Risotto 10

Arizona Yellow Risotto 11

Hot Couscous Risotto 12

Josephine's Risotto 13

Lemon Pepper Cookout Risotto 14

Yam Risotto 15

Fruit Risotto 16

Twin City Suburb Risotto 17

Risotto Kerala Style 18

Sweet Bavarian Risotto 19

Hot Tuna Risotto 20

Parmesan Pesto Risotto 21

Slow Cooker Risotto 22

Simple Long Grain Risotto 23

Risotto Alaska 24

Summer Celery Risotto 25

Hot Salami Risotto 26

Spanish Risotto con Azafran 27

Zucchini Risotto 28

Moroccan Lamb Risotto 29

Mediterranean Veal Risotto 30

New England Ginger Risotto 32

Oriental Risotto 33

English Tuna Risotto 34

Mushroom Florets Risotto 35

Holiday Risotto 36

September's Quinoa Risotto 37

August's Quinoa Risotto 38

Gilroy Garlic Risotto 39

5-Ingredient Seafood Risotto 40

Risotto with Scallops 41

Simple Pesto 42

Risotto Chicken Dinner 43

Roasted Mozzarella Risotto 44

Italian Risotto 45

25-Minute Chicken Risotto 46

True Country Risotto 47

Dijon Beef Risotto 48

Seattle Vegetable Risotto 49

Late October Pine Nut Risotto 50

Oyster Mushroom and Barley Risotto 51

Oven Roasted Risotto 52

Zesty Summer Risotto 53

Pittsburgh Style Risotto 54

Fathia's Favorite Risotto 55

Romano Mushroom 56

Cream of Risotto 57

New York Style Risotto 58

Spinach Risotto 59

Risotto 101 60

Risotto Persian 61

African Quinoa "Risotto" 62

Nana's Asiago "Risotto" 63

Mediterranean Risotto Greek Style 64

Simple French Style Risotto 65

How to Make a Risotto 66

Tallahassee Seafood Risotto 67

Risotto Brasileiro 68

Caprese Risotto 69

No Rice Risotto 70

Picnic Risotto 71

Minty Garden Risotto 72

Wisconsin Country Risotto 73

New Hampshire Restaurant Risotto 74

Mediterranean Lentil Risotto 75

Full Veggie Risotto 76

South American Kidney Beans Risotto 77

Downstate Risotto 78

Easy Peasey Risotto 79

Savory Cinnamon Risotto 80

Italian Herbed Risotto 81

Amish Barley Risotto 82

South of the Border Risotto 83

New Mexican Mesa Risotto 84

Risotto Roots 85

California Risotto 86

Butternut Bacon Risotto 87

Risotto Hot Pot 88

Tuscan Risotto 89

Rice Cooker Risotto 90

Autumn Sunset Risotto 91

Weekend Risotto Casserole 92

Weeknight Risotto Bowls 93

Central American Risotto 94

Simple Homemade Red Curry Paste 95

Sonoma
Orzo Risotto

🥣 Prep Time: 15 mins
🕐 Total Time: 30 mins

Servings per Recipe: 4

Calories	297.7
Fat	10.1g
Cholesterol	5.5mg
Sodium	358.8mg
Carbohydrates	39.4g
Protein	14.9g

Ingredients

2 tsp olive oil
2 garlic cloves, chopped
1/2 medium onion, chopped
1 lb. mushroom, chopped chunks
3 tbsp pine nuts
1 C. orzo pasta
2 C. low sodium chicken broth

1/2 tsp ground sage
1/4 tsp ground thyme
1/4 C. grated parmesan cheese
1/2 tsp kosher salt
ground pepper

Directions

1. Place a large saucepan over medium heat. Heat in it the oil.
2. Cook in it the garlic with onion for 3 min. Stir in the mushrooms with a pinch of salt.
3. Cook them for 4 min. Stir in the sage with thyme and broth. Cook them until they start boiling.
4. Stir in the orzo and lower the heat. Let them cook for 16 min while stirring often.
5. One the time is up, stir in the pine nuts, parmesan cheese, and parsley.
6. Cook them for extra few minutes until the cheese melts. Serve your risotto immediately.
7. Enjoy.

RISOTTO
Mexicana

Prep Time: 15 mins
Total Time: 1 hr 15 mins

Servings per Recipe: 4

Calories	495.5
Fat	21.2g
Cholesterol	0.0mg
Sodium	110.5mg
Carbohydrates	63.3g
Protein	16.2g

Ingredients

4 tbsp olive oil
1 onion, chopped
2 garlic cloves, chopped
3/4 C. brown rice
2 1/2 C. vegetable stock
salt and pepper
1 red bell pepper, seeded and chopped
2 celery ribs, sliced

8 oz. cremini mushrooms, sliced
1 (15 oz.) cans red kidney beans
3 tbsp parsley, chopped
3/8 C. cashews

Directions

1. Place a large skillet over medium heat. Heat in it half of the oil.
2. Cook in it the onion for 4 min. Stir in 1 clove of garlic and cook them for 3 min.
3. Stir in the rice and cook them for 2 min. Stir in the stock with a pinch of salt and pepper.
4. Cook them until they start boiling while stirring. Lower the heat and put on the lid.
5. Let the risotto cook for 36 to 42 min.
6. Place pan over medium heat. Heat in it the remaining oil. Cook in it the celery with bell pepper for 6 min.
7. Stir in the mushrooms with the rest of the garlic. Cook them for 4 min while stirring.
8. Add the cooked rice with beans, cashews, and parsley. Cook them for 2 to 3 min while stirring.
9. Adjust the seasoning of your risotto then serve it warm.
10. Enjoy.

Vegan
Dessert Risotto

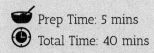 Prep Time: 5 mins

Total Time: 40 mins

Servings per Recipe: 4
Calories   104.8
Fat   0.1g
Cholesterol   0.0mg
Sodium   1.3mg
Carbohydrates   24.5g
Protein   1.2g

Ingredients

7 oz. risotto rice
2 tbsp sugar
1 1/2 C. vanilla-flavored rice milk,
warmed
1/2 C. apple juice, unsweetened
1/2 tsp cinnamon
1/8 tsp ground vanilla bean

Additions
fresh fruit etc.

Directions

1. Before you do anything, preheat the oven to 350 F.
2. Get a baking dish and coat it with oil. Stir in it the sugar with rice, milk, and spics.
3. Layover it a piece of foil to cover it then cook it for 26 min in the oven.
4. Once the time is up, top your risotto with your favorite fruit.
5. Cook it for an extra 11 min then serve it warm.
6. Enjoy.

ALLEGHANY
Mushroom Risotto

Prep Time: 15 mins
Total Time: 1 hr 5 mins

Servings per Recipe: 6
Calories	305.5
Fat	11.6g
Cholesterol	29.9mg
Sodium	743.2mg
Carbohydrates	36.3g
Protein	12.9g

Ingredients

3 tbsp butter
2 C. mushrooms, sliced
1/2 C. onion, chopped
1 1/4 C. Arborio rice
3 1/2 C. chicken broth

1 C. parmesan cheese, shredded
2 tbsp thyme, chopped

Directions

1. Before you do anything, preheat the oven to 375 F.
2. Place a large ovenproof pan over medium heat. Heat in it the butter.
3. Cook in it the mushrooms with onion for 6 min. Add the rice and cook them for 1 min.
4. Add the broth with a pinch of salt and pepper. Put on the lid and place the pan in the oven for 46 min.
5. Once the time is up, turn off the heat and add the cheese with thyme.
6. Serve your risotto warm.
7. Enjoy.

Arizona
Yellow Risotto

🥣 Prep Time: 10 mins
🕐 Total Time: 40 mins

Servings per Recipe: 4
Calories	217.8
Fat	21.1g
Cholesterol	68.5mg
Sodium	149.3mg
Carbohydrates	3.3g
Protein	4.8g

Ingredients

2 tbsp butter
1/2 C. sliced mushrooms
1/2 C. chopped onion
2 1/2 C. water
1 (8 oz.) packages Yellow Rice

1/2 C. heavy cream
1/2 C. shredded Monterey jack cheese
1 C. baby spinach leaves

Directions

1. Place a large saucepan over medium heat. Heat in it the butter.
2. Cook in it the mushrooms for 3 min. Add the rice mix with water.
3. Cook them until they start boiling while stirring it often. Lower the heat and put on the lid.
4. Let it cook for 22 min. Once the time is up, add the cream with cheese, a pinch of salt and pepper.
5. Cook them or an extra 4 min. Add the spinach and put on the lid.
6. Turn off the heat and let the risotto rest for 6 min. Serve it immediately.
7. Enjoy.

HOT
Couscous Risotto

Prep Time: 10 mins
Total Time: 30 mins

Servings per Recipe: 4

Calories	334.3
Fat	7.6g
Cholesterol	0.0mg
Sodium	24.2mg
Carbohydrates	56.6g
Protein	10.1g

Ingredients

2 C. low sodium vegetable broth
2 tbsp olive oil, divided
6 oz. shiitake mushrooms, sliced
1 poblano chile, diced
2 shallots, minced
1 carrot, diced

1 (8 7/8 oz.) boxes Israeli couscous
1/2 peas
3 tbsp chives, chopped
2 tbsp fresh tarragon, chopped

Directions

1. Place a large saucepan over high heat. Heat in it 4 C. of water until they start boiling.
2. Place a pot over medium heat. Heat in it 1 tbsp of oil. Cook in it the poblano with mushrooms for 6 min.
3. Drain them and place them aside. Stir the carrots into the same pot and cook them for 4 min.
4. Stir in the couscous and cook them for an extra 2 min.
5. Lower the heat and stir in 1/4 C. of broth. Cook them while stirring until the couscous absorbs it.
6. Repeat the process with the remaining broth until the couscous absorbs all of it.
7. Stir in the peas with cooked mushrooms and poblano. Cook them for 3 min.
8. Add 3 tbsp of chives with tarragon, a pinch of salt and pepper. Serve your risotto warm.
9. Enjoy.

Josephine's
Risotto

Prep Time: 5 mins
Total Time: 20 mins

Servings per Recipe: 6
Calories	823.9
Fat	44.6g
Cholesterol	117.1mg
Sodium	1043.7mg
Carbohydrates	73.7g
Protein	30.7g

Ingredients

17.5 oz. round short-grain rice
6 C. water
5 oz. butter
2 large onions, minced
10.5 oz. parmesan cheese, grated
5 oz. goat cheese, cubed

9 oz. turkey, sliced, optional
1/2 tsp fresh rosemary
1 tbsp olive oil
pepper
salt

Directions

1. Place a large saucepan over medium heat. Heat in it the oil.
2. Cook in it the pepper with onion for 3 min. Stir in the rice and cook them for 1 min.
3. Add the rice and bring them to a rolling boil for 12 min.
4. Stir in the butter with rosemary, parmesan cheese, goat cheese, a pinch of salt and pepper.
5. Garnish your risotto with turkey then serve it.
6. Enjoy.

LEMON
Pepper Cookout Risotto

🥣 Prep Time: 30 mins

🕐 Total Time: 47 mins

Servings per Recipe: 4

Calories	626.0
Fat	29.0g
Cholesterol	69.4mg
Sodium	1491.5mg
Carbohydrates	61.3g
Protein	27.9g

Ingredients

Marinade
1/4 C. olive oil
1 tsp sea salt
1/4 tsp red pepper flakes
1/4 tsp dried rosemary
1/2 tsp oregano
1/4 tsp lemon pepper
2 large boneless skinless chicken breasts
Rice
3 quarts water
1 1/2 C. Arborio rice
1 tsp salt
1 C. mozzarella cheese, shredded
1/4 C. parmesan cheese, shredded
1 tbsp unsalted butter
2 C. baby arugula
1 C. mushroom, sliced
1 tbsp olive oil
black pepper

Directions

1. Get a large mixing bowl: Stir in it all the marinade ingredients.
2. Stir in the chicken breasts and poke them all over with a fork. Let them sit for 35 min.
3. Before you do anything, preheat the grill and grease it.
4. Drain the chicken breasts and grill them for 6 to 8 min on each side.
5. Cover them with a piece of foil and place them aside.
6. Place a large pot over medium heat. Bring in it the water to a boil.
7. Cook in it the rice with a pinch of salt until they start boiling. Keep it boiling for 16 to 18 min while stirring.
8. Place a skillet over medium heat. Heat in it the olive oil. Cook in it the mushroom for 5 min.
9. Strain the rice and add it the same skillet with cheese, butter, and arugula. Cook them until the cheese melts. Top your risotto with grilled chicken then serve them warm. Enjoy.

Yam
Risotto

Prep Time: 5 mins
Total Time: 30 mins

Servings per Recipe: 4
Calories	429.4
Fat	21.9g
Cholesterol	41.5mg
Sodium	292.1mg
Carbohydrates	48.8g
Protein	9.6g

Ingredients

4 tbsp butter
2 tbsp minced shallots
1 medium sweet potato, cubed
1/3 C. chopped pecans
2 - 3 C. vegetable broth
1 C. Arborio rice

salt & ground black pepper
1/2 C. grated parmesan cheese
1 tbsp chopped green onion tops

Directions

1. Place a large saucepan over medium heat. Bring in it the broth to a boil.
2. Place a pot over medium heat. Heat in it the butter. Cook in it the pecans with shallot for 4 min.
3. Stir in the rice and cook them for 2 min. Add the sweet potato with 3/4 C. of boiling broth.
4. Let them cook until the rice absorbs the broth while stirring.
5. Repeat the process with the remaining broth until the rice absorbs all of it and becomes creamy.
6. Add the green onion with cheese, a pinch of salt and pepper. Serve your risotto warm.
7. Enjoy.

FRUIT
Risotto

Prep Time: 15 mins

Total Time: 45 mins

Servings per Recipe: 4
Calories	289.7
Fat	7.3g
Cholesterol	16.3mg
Sodium	443.5mg
Carbohydrates	51.2g
Protein	5.7g

Ingredients

2 tbsp butter
3 garlic cloves, roasted
1 small onion, diced
3/4 C. Arborio rice
2 C. chicken broth

3/4 C. dried sweetened cranberries
1 tbsp parmesan cheese

Directions

1. Before you do anything, preheat the oven to 400 F.
2. Coat a baking dish with some oil. Place it aside.
3. Place a pot over medium heat. Heat in it the butter. Cook in it the onion with garlic for 2 min.
4. Stir in the rice and cook them for 1 min. Stir in the broth with cranberries.
5. Cook them until they start boiling. Spoon the mixture into the greased pan.
6. Place it in the oven and let it cook for 26 min. Add the cheese then serve it.
7. Enjoy.

Twin City
Suburb Risotto

🥣 Prep Time: 5 mins
🕐 Total Time: 45 mins

Servings per Recipe: 4
Calories	823.7
Fat	42.6g
Cholesterol	74.9mg
Sodium	1688.4mg
Carbohydrates	69.6g
Protein	39.4g

Ingredients

2 tbsp extra virgin olive oil
1 lb. Italian chicken sausage, sweet, casings removed
1 onion, large, sliced
1 garlic clove, large, minced
1 1/2 C. orzo pasta
2 C. chicken stock
salt and pepper

1 C. marinated artichoke drained and quartered
1 C. frozen baby peas
3 tbsp chives, snipped
6 tbsp parmesan cheese, grated parmesan cheese

Directions

1. Place a large pan over medium heat. Heat in it the oil.
2. Cook in it the sausage for 6 min. Drain it and place it aside.
3. Lower the heat and stir the garlic with onion into the same pan.
4. Put on the lid and let them cook for 5 min. Stir in the orzo and let them cook for 2 min.
5. Stir in 2 C. of water with stock, a pinch of salt and pepper.
6. Cook them for 16 min while stirring often until the risotto becomes creamy.
7. Stir in the sausage, artichokes, peas, chives, and parmesan. Cook them for 5 min.
8. Serve your risotto hot.
9. Enjoy.

RISOTTO
Kerala Style

Prep Time: 10 mins
Total Time: 40 mins

Servings per Recipe: 8

Calories	386.3
Fat	9.5g
Cholesterol	17.0mg
Sodium	248.9mg
Carbohydrates	63.8g
Protein	11.9g

Ingredients

1 tbsp grapeseed oil
1 tbsp sesame oil
15 curry leaves, washed, dried, and julienned
2 green chilies, washed, dried, and sliced
2 tbsp cumin seeds
1 tbsp black mustard seeds
2 onions, diced

8 oz. mushrooms, diced
4 carrots, peeled and grated
2 C. jasmine rice, uncooked
4 C. of warm milk
15 oz. chickpeas, canned
salt

Directions

1. Place a large saucepan over medium heat. Stir in it the grapeseed oil, sesame oil, curry leaves and green chilies.
2. Cook them for 1 min. Stir in the cumin seeds and mustard seeds. Cook them for an extra 2 min.
3. Stir in the onions, mushrooms, and carrots. Cook them for 4 min.
4. Stir in the rice with a pinch of salt and pepper. Cook them for 3 min while stirring.
5. Add the milk gradually while stirring until the rice becomes creamy.
6. Stir in the chickpeas with a pinch of salt and pepper.
7. Garnish your risotto with some cilantro, chopped fresh onions, tomatoes, cucumber, yogurt and raita then serve it.
8. Enjoy.

Sweet
Bavarian Risotto

Prep Time: 2 mins
Total Time: 12 mins

Servings per Recipe: 4
Calories   396.5
Fat   20.0g
Cholesterol   44.1mg
Sodium   41.0mg
Carbohydrates   52.7g
Protein   5.1g

Ingredients

1 C. White Rice, uncooked
1 C. milk
1/3 C. sugar
2 tbsp unsalted butter

1/4 C. heavy cream
1/2 C. semi-sweet chocolate chips

Directions

1. Place a large saucepan over medium heat. Stir in the sugar with milk, rice and a pinch of salt.
2. Cook them until they start boiling. Turn off the heat and put on the lid.
3. Let the risotto rest for 6 min. Add the cream with chocolate chips and butter.
4. Adjust the seasoning of your risotto then serve it.
5. Enjoy.

HOT
Tuna Risotto

Prep Time: 10 mins
Total Time: 40 mins

Servings per Recipe: 4
Calories	463.3
Fat	6.1g
Cholesterol	46.2mg
Sodium	730.6mg
Carbohydrates	64.9g
Protein	33.7g

Ingredients

1 1/4 C. Arborio rice
4 C. chicken stock
13 oz. canned tuna, slices in spring water
1 onion, chopped
1/4 C. stock, extra
1 - 2 tsp chili, minced
1 tbsp lemon juice

1 lemon, zest of
3/4 C. frozen peas
1 tbsp of oil
parmesan cheese

Directions

1. Place a large deep pan over medium heat. Heat in it the oil.
2. Cook in it the onion with chili and rice for 2 min. Stir 1 C. of stock and heat them until they start boiling.
3. Lower the heat and let them cook while stirring often until the rice absorbs it.
4. Repeat the process with the remaining broth until the risotto becomes creamy.
5. Stir in the peas, tuna and lemon juice and zest. Heat them for 2 min. Serve it warm.
6. Enjoy.

Parmesan
Pesto Risotto

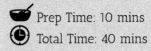

Prep Time: 10 mins
Total Time: 40 mins

Servings per Recipe: 2
Calories	363.5
Fat	10.0g
Cholesterol	24.2mg
Sodium	482.3mg
Carbohydrates	55.2g
Protein	14.0g

Ingredients

1 C. risotto rice (Arborio)
2 1/2 C. chicken stock
1 tbsp butter
1 red bell pepper, chopped
1 onion, chopped
1 tomatoes, chopped
1/2 zucchini, chopped
1/3 C. peas

1/2 C. mushroom, sliced
2 - 3 tbsp pesto sauce, see appendix
parmesan cheese, grated
salt and pepper

Directions

1. Place a pot deep pan over medium heat. Heat in it the butter. Cook in it the onion for 2 min.
2. Stir in the pepper and cook them for 2 min. Lower the heat and stir in the rice.
3. Cook them for 1 min. Stir in 1/4 C. of bouillon and cook them until the rice absorbs it while stirring.
4. Stir in the tomato with zucchini. Cook them for 22 min while stirring adding more broth when needed.
5. Stir in the mushrooms with a pinch of salt and pepper. Cook them for 5 min while stirring.
6. Stir in the peas with any bouillon left. Season them with a pinch of salt and pepper.
7. Serve your risotto warm with toppings of your choice.
8. Enjoy.

SLOW COOKER
Risotto

Prep Time: 15 mins
Total Time: 8 hrs 15 mins

Servings per Recipe: 4

Calories	359.4
Fat	2.6g
Cholesterol	0.0mg
Sodium	44.3mg
Carbohydrates	77.2g
Protein	9.0g

Ingredients

1/2 tbsp olive oil
2 - 2 1/2 onions, chopped
1 tsp minced garlic
1/2 tsp dried rosemary
1 1/2 C. pearl barley

3 C. vegetable stock
2 sweet potatoes, peeled and chopped

Directions

1. Place a large pan over medium heat. Heat in it the oil.
2. Cook in it the onion for 2 min. Stir in the garlic with rosemary. Cook them for 1 min.
3. add the barley and cook them for 2 min. Stir in the stock and cook them until they start boiling.
4. Spoon the mixture to a stockpot. Add the sweet potato and put on the lid.
5. Let them cook for 7 to 8 h on low.
6. Adjust the seasoning of your risotto then serve it warm.
7. Enjoy.

Simple
Long Grain Risotto

Prep Time: 15 mins
Total Time: 35 mins

Servings per Recipe: 4
Calories	153.0
Fat	2.1g
Cholesterol	5.8mg
Sodium	677.5mg
Carbohydrates	27.5g
Protein	5.2g

Ingredients

1/3 C. onion, chopped
1 tbsp garlic, minced
2/3 C. long grain rice
2 C. water
2 tsp instant chicken bouillon granules

1/4 tsp black pepper, ground
1/4 C. parmesan cheese, grated

Directions

1. Place a large saucepan over medium heat. Heat in it the butter.
2. Cook in it the onion with garlic for 3 min. Stir in the rice and cook them for 1 min.
3. Add the water with bouillon granules. Cook them until they start boiling.
4. Lower the heat and put on the lid. Let them cook for 22 to 26 min.
5. Turn off the heat and stir in the cheese until the risotto becomes creamy.
6. Serve it immediately.
7. Enjoy.

RISOTTO
Alaska

Prep Time: 10 mins
Total Time: 30 mins

Servings per Recipe: 2
Calories	580.6
Fat	20.1g
Cholesterol	220.4mg
Sodium	494.0mg
Carbohydrates	21.7g
Protein	73.1g

Ingredients

2 fresh salmon fillets
3 oz. shrimp
1 vegetable stock cube
5 oz. risotto rice
1 pint boiling water
2 bay leaves
2 tbsp crème fraiche
2 tsp dried dill

1 tsp dried herbs
lemon juice
lemon zest
olive oil
salt and pepper

Directions

1. Place a large deep pan over medium heat. Heat in it the oil.
2. Cook in it the dry herbs with bay leaf, and rice. Cook them for 6 min.
3. Stir in 1/3 C. of stock and cook them for 6 min while stirring.
4. Repeat the process with the remaining stock until the all of it is absorbed.
5. Place a skillet of over medium heat: Stir in 1 tbsp olive oil, lemon zest, crème fraiche and dill.
6. Heat them for 2 min. Add the salmon fillets and cook them for 4 to 6 min on each side.
7. Flake it and place it aside.
8. Stir the lemon juice with shrimp, a pinch of salt and pepper into the risotto.
9. Cook them for 6 min. Discard the bay leaves and stir in the salmon. Serve it immediately.
10. Enjoy.

Summer
Celery Risotto

Prep Time: 15 mins
Total Time: 45 mins

Servings per Recipe: 4
Calories	363.5
Fat	10.0g
Cholesterol	24.2mg
Sodium	482.3mg
Carbohydrates	55.2g
Protein	14.0g

Ingredients

2 tbsp butter
3 shallots, chopped
2 sticks celery, chopped
1 tbsp extra virgin olive oil
2 C. Arborio rice
1 1/2-2 liters vegetable stock
1 lemon, zest
1/4 C. lemon juice, squeezed

1 tsp dried rosemary
6 tbsp parmesan cheese, grated
1/3 C. heavy cream
2 tbsp butter
salt and pepper

Directions

1. Get a mixing bowl: Stir in it the lemon juice, cream, and parmesan.
2. Place a large pan over medium heat. Heat in it the oil with 2 tbsp of butter.
3. Cook in it the celery with shallot for 4 min. Stir in the rice and cook them for 1 min.
4. Stir in 1 C. of stock. Cook them until the rice absorbs it.
5. Repeat the process with the remaining broth until the rice is done.
6. Stir in the lemon zest and rosemary.
7. Remove the pan from the heat and add to it the butter with a pinch of salt and pepper.
8. Serve your risotto immediately.
9. Enjoy.

HOT
Salami Risotto

Prep Time: 10 mins
Total Time: 15 mins

Servings per Recipe: 4

Calories	510.0
Fat	18.4g
Cholesterol	28.7mg
Sodium	704.3mg
Carbohydrates	71.3g
Protein	14.7g

Ingredients

2 tbsp olive oil
1 large onion, chopped
1 1/2 C. Arborio rice
15 oz. tomatoes
3 C. water
3.5 oz. spicy beef salami, chopped
1/4 C. sun-dried tomato, drained and sliced

1/2 C. black olives, seeded and sliced
1 tsp dried chili pepper flakes
1/2 C. grated parmesan cheese

Directions

1. Place a large skillet over medium heat. Heat in it the oil.
2. Cook in it the onion for 3 min. Stir in the rice and cook them for 2 min.
3. Stir in the tomatoes with water. Cook them until they start boiling.
4. Lower the heat and put on the lid. Cook them for 16 min.
5. Turn off the heat and let the risotto rest for 12 min.
6. Add the chili flakes with olives, dried tomato, cheese, and salami. Serve it warm.
7. Enjoy.

Spanish
Risotto con Azafran

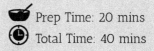 Prep Time: 20 mins

Total Time: 40 mins

Servings per Recipe: 4
Calories	446.7
Fat	9.7g
Cholesterol	96.2mg
Sodium	707.3mg
Carbohydrates	65.7g
Protein	23.4g

Ingredients

8 oz. peas
4 oz. zucchini, sliced
2 tbsp olive oil
1 onion, chopped
1/2 tsp saffron thread
4 oz. Arborio rice
4 cloves garlic, crushed
8 oz. button mushrooms, sliced

1 lemon, juice and rind
3 C. fish stock
10.5 oz. cooked prawns, peeled, tails intact
3 tbsp chopped flat leaf parsley

Directions

1. Bring a large saucepan of water to a boil. Cook in it the zucchini with peas for 2 min.
2. Drain them, dip them in cold water and drain them again.
3. Place a large skillet over medium heat. Heat in it the oil.
4. Cook in it the onion with saffron for 3 min. Stir in the rice, garlic, and mushrooms.
5. Cook them for 3 min. Stir in the lemon rind with 1/3 of the stock while stirring.
6. Cook them until the rice absorbs it. Repeat the process with the remaining stock until the rice becomes creamy.
7. Stir in the prawns, blanched vegetables, and lemon juice. Season them with a pinch of salt and pepper.
8. Cook them for 2 min. Add the parsley and serve it warm.
9. Enjoy.

ZUCCHINI
Risotto

Prep Time: 10 mins
Total Time: 25 mins

Servings per Recipe: 4

Calories	292.9
Fat	9.0g
Cholesterol	15.8mg
Sodium	199.8mg
Carbohydrates	40.8g
Protein	13.1g

Ingredients

1 small zucchini, chopped
1 shallot, chopped
1 tbsp olive oil
2 garlic cloves, minced
1 C. orzo pasta
2 C. vegetable broth
1 C. milk
6 oz. spinach

2 tomatoes, chopped
1/4 C. basil
1/3 C. parmesan cheese
1/4 tsp salt and pepper

Directions

1. Place a pot over medium heat. Heat in it the oil. Cook in it the zucchini with shallot for 3 min.
2. Stir in the garlic and cook them for 2 min. Stir in the orzo, broth, and milk.
3. Cook them until they start boiling. Lower the heat and let it cook for 12 to 16 min while stirring.
4. Once the time is up, add the basil with tomato, spinach, a pinch of salt and pepper.
5. Cook them for 3 min. Turn off the heat and add the cheese. Serve your risotto right away.
6. Enjoy.

Moroccan
Lamb Risotto

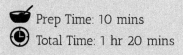

Prep Time: 10 mins
Total Time: 1 hr 20 mins

Servings per Recipe: 6
Calories   231.0
Fat   13.1g
Cholesterol   10.1mg
Sodium   44.0mg
Carbohydrates   26.1g
Protein   3.7g

Ingredients

Lamb Sausage
6 large fresh lamb sausages
water, for boiling
1 tbsp canola oil
fresh rosemary sprig
Risotto
4 large Yukon gold potatoes, diced cubes
salt
3 tbsp extra-virgin olive oil

1 large shallot, minced
3 C. stock
6 large fresh mushrooms, sliced
kosher salt & ground black pepper
1 C. loosely packed grated Parmigiano
2 - 4 tbsp butter
baby arugula

Directions

1. To prepare the sausages:
2. Bring a large salted saucepan of water to a boil. Cook in it the sausages for 7 min.
3. Drain it and place it aside.
4. Place a skillet over medium heat. Heat in it the oil. Cook in it the rosemary needles for 30 sec.
5. Stir in the sausages and cook them for 6 in. Drain them and place them aside.
6. To prepare the risotto:
7. Bring a large salted pot of water to a boil. Cook in it the potatoes for 6 min. Drain them.
8. Place a pot over medium heat. Heat in it the oil. Cook in it the shallot with potatoes, a pinch of salt and pepper for 3 min.
9. Stir in a ladle of stock and cook them until it is absorbed. Repeat the process with the remaining stock until all of it is absorbed.
10. Place a skillet over medium heat. Heat in it a drizzle of olive oil.
11. Cook in it the mushrooms for 8 min. Stir them into the risotto with cheese, butter, a pinch of salt and pepper. Spoon the sausage on top then serve it warm Enjoy.

MEDITERRANEAN
Veal Risotto

Prep Time: 10 mins
Total Time: 45 mins

Servings per Recipe: 4	
Calories	1010.1
Fat	51.0g
Cholesterol	119.9mg
Sodium	1144.0mg
Carbohydrates	115.0g
Protein	24.8g

Ingredients

Risotto
4 C. chicken stock
1 onion, chopped
1 tbsp olive oil
2 C. Arborio rice
1/4 C. butter
1 C. feta cheese, grated
1 C. feta cheese, cubed
4 C. spinach
1 lemon, juice and zest
Shrimp
1 tbsp canola oil
12 large shrimp, cleaned and deveined,
tail intact
2 tbsp ouzo
2 tbsp butter
sea salt & ground black pepper
1/4 C. fresh parsley, chopped

Stock
8 meaty veal bones, chopped
3 tbsp canola oil
sea salt & ground black pepper
1 tbsp tomato paste
1 head garlic
6 carrots
2 onions
4 stalks celery
2 large leeks
4 sprigs fresh thyme
4 sprigs fresh rosemary
4 large sprigs fresh flat-leaf parsley
17 C. water

Directions

1. To prepare the stock:
2. Before you do anything, preheat the oven to 450 F.
3. Place a meat on in a roasting dish. Top them with the bones, a drizzle of olive oil, salt, and pepper.
4. Place the pan in the oven and let them cook for 30 min. Stir them and cook them for an extra 30 min.
5. Once the time is up, stir in the tomato paste with veggies. Cook them for another 60 min.

6. Transfer the mixture to a large pot. Stir in the water with herbs, a pinch of salt and pepper.
7. Stir 1/2 C. of water into the roasting pan, stir it and add it to the pot.
8. Cook them until they start boiling. Lower the heat and put on the lid.
9. Let the stock cook for 8 h while adding water if needed and skimming the fat every once in a while.
10. Once the time is up, strain the stock and discard the fat. Place it aside to cool down completely.
11. Pour it into airtight containers and freeze them until ready to use.
12. To prepare the risotto:
13. Place a pot over medium heat. Heat in it the oil.
14. Cook in it the onion for 4 min. Stir in the rice and cook them for 1 min.
15. Stir in 3/4 C. of broth and cook them while stirring until the rice absorbs it.
16. Repeat the process with the remaining stock while stirring until the risotto becomes creamy over low heat.
17. Once the time is up, stir in the cheeses with butter. Cook them for 1 min.
18. Stir in the spinach and the lemon juice. Adjust the seasoning of your risotto and place it aside.
19. To prepare the shrimp:
20. Place a large pan over medium heat. Heat in it the oil.
21. Cook in it the shrimp for 3 to 4 min. Season it with a pinch of salt and pepper.
22. Arrange it over the risotto then serve it warm.
23. Enjoy.

NEW ENGLAND
Ginger Risotto

Prep Time: 20 mins

Total Time: 25 mins

Servings per Recipe: 4

Calories	367.5
Fat	5.5g
Cholesterol	234.2mg
Sodium	2230.7mg
Carbohydrates	55.0g
Protein	21.1g

Ingredients

4 C. hot cooked rice

7 oz. canned crabmeat

4 eggs

1 scallion

4 C. dashi

2 tbsp white vinegar

2 tsp salt

3 tbsp light soy sauce

1 tbsp fresh ginger juice

1/4 sheet nori

Directions

1. Remove the white tendons from the crab meat. Use a fork to flake them.
2. Place a large saucepan over medium heat. Stir in it the dashi with spices.
3. Cook them until they start boiling. Stir in the crabmeat with rice. Bring them to another boil.
4. Lower the heat and let them cook for 3 to 4 min. Stir in the ginger juice with beaten eggs while stirring.
5. Cook them for 1 to 2 min. Turn off the heat and put on the lid.
6. Spoon the risotto into the serving bowl. Top them with nori and serve them.
7. Enjoy.

Oriental
Risotto

Prep Time: 10 mins
Total Time: 50 mins

Servings per Recipe: 6
Calories	370.8
Fat	9.3g
Cholesterol	46.7mg
Sodium	129.6mg
Carbohydrates	53.4g
Protein	17.6g

Ingredients

2 - 3 leeks, sliced and divided
4 C. almond breeze milk
1 - 2 tbsp Thai red curry paste, see appendix
1 tbsp dried unsweetened coconut
2 boneless skinless chicken breasts, cubed
1 tsp coconut oil
1 garlic clove, minced

2 red sliced bell peppers
1 1/2 C. Arborio rice
1 bunch chopped basil

Directions

1. Place a large saucepan over high heat. Stir in it half of the leeks with Almond Breeze Unsweetened Original, Thai paste and dried coconut.
2. Cook them until they start boiling. Stir in the chicken breasts and cook them for 7 to 9 min.
3. Place a large saucepan over medium heat. Heat in it the oil.
4. Cook in it the remaining leeks with peppers and garlic for 6 min.
5. Add the rice and cook them for 2 min. Stir in the chicken mixture. Lower the heat and put on the lid.
6. Cook the risotto for 14 to 16 min while stirring from time to time.
7. Adjust the seasoning of your risotto then serve it warm.
8. Enjoy.

ENGLISH
Tuna Risotto

Prep Time: 10 mins
Total Time: 50 mins

Servings per Recipe: 4
Calories	186.3
Fat	8.4g
Cholesterol	24.2mg
Sodium	576.8mg
Carbohydrates	18.7g
Protein	8.6g

Ingredients

Tuna
4 tuna steaks
1 tbsp Worcestershire sauce
1 tsp salt and pepper
1 tbsp lemon juice
Risotto
1 C. risotto rice
2 C. chicken broth

2 C. water
1 onion, diced
1 garlic clove, crushed
1 tbsp butter
3/4 C. shredded mozzarella cheese
2 tbsp lemon juice

Directions

1. To prepare the risotto:
2. Place a large skillet over medium heat. Heat in it the butter.
3. Cook in it the onion for 3 min. Stir in the rice and cook them for 1 min. Lower the heat and stir in ½ C. broth and 2 tbsp lemon juice until the rice absorbs it. Repeat the process with the remaining broth and water until all of it is absorbed while stirring.
4. Cook them until the risotto is creamy.
5. To prepare the tuna:
6. Get a mixing bowl: Whisk in it the Worcestershire sauce and lemon juice. Coat the tuna steaks with the mixture. Season them with a pinch of salt and pepper.
7. Place a large skillet over medium heat. Heat in it the oil.
8. Cook in it the steaks for 2 to 3 min on each side. Serve them warm with the risotto.
9. Enjoy.

Mushroom
Florets Risotto

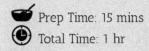 Prep Time: 15 mins

Total Time: 1 hr

Servings per Recipe: 4

Calories	238.3
Fat	15.4g
Cholesterol	24.9mg
Sodium	628.5mg
Carbohydrates	12.3g
Protein	15.0g

Ingredients

1 onion, sliced
4 oz. mushrooms, sliced
2 tbsp extra virgin olive oil, divided
1 cauliflower head, riced
1/4 C. flat leaf parsley, chopped
1 tbsp fresh rosemary, chopped

4 oz. parmesan cheese, grated
1 C. almond milk
1/4 tsp salt
1/4 tsp pepper

Directions

1. Before you do anything, preheat the oven to 350 F.
2. Place a large skillet over medium heat. Heat in it 1 tbsp of EVOO.
3. Cook in it the onion for 3 min. Turn off the heat.
4. Get a mixing bowl: Toss in it the herbs with cauliflower and Evoo. Pour the mixture into a baking sheet.
5. Cook them in the oven for 32 min.
6. In the meantime, place a pan over medium heat.
7. Stir in it the baked cauliflower with onion, mushroom, cheese, milk, a pinch of salt and pepper.
8. Cook them until they start boiling. Lower the heat and let them cook for 6 min. Serve it warm.
9. Enjoy.

HOLIDAY
Risotto

Prep Time: 20 mins
Total Time: 1 hr

Servings per Recipe: 4
Calories	506.1
Fat	15.1g
Cholesterol	5.5mg
Sodium	109.7mg
Carbohydrates	83.6g
Protein	12.1g

Ingredients

3 lb. pumpkin, peeled and diced
2 tbsp oil
4 C. of boiling vegetable stock
1 onion, diced
2 garlic cloves, crushed
1 1/2 C. Arborio rice
1 1/2 C. baby spinach leaves
1/4 C. parmesan cheese

1/4 C. pine nuts, toasted
extra grated parmesan cheese

Directions

1. Before you do anything, preheat the oven to 400 F.
2. Put the pumpkin in a baking pan. Cook it in the oven for 22 min.
3. Place a large saucepan over medium heat. Heat in it the oil.
4. Cook in it the garlic with onion for 6 min. Add the rice and cook them for 1 min.
5. Stir 1 C. of boiling stock. Cook them until the rice absorbs while stirring.
6. Repeat the process with the remaining stock until all of it is absorbed.
7. Add the cheese with pine nuts, pumpkin, spinach, a pinch of salt and pepper. Serve it warm.
8. Enjoy.

September's
Quinoa Risotto

🥣 Prep Time: 15 mins

🕐 Total Time: 30 mins

Servings per Recipe: 4

Calories	196.1
Fat	6.1g
Cholesterol	0.0mg
Sodium	584.7mg
Carbohydrates	29.3g
Protein	6.3g

Ingredients

1 tbsp olive oil
1 C. quinoa
1/2 onion, chopped
1 garlic clove, chopped
1 tsp ginger, chopped
2 C. vegetable broth
2 tsp curry powder
3 C. vegetables, diced

1 tsp salt
1 dash cayenne

Directions

1. Place a large skillet over medium heat. Heat in it the oil.
2. Cook in it the onions, garlic, and ginger for 3 min. Stir in the quinoa and cook them for 2 min.
3. Stir in the broth and cook them until they start boiling. Lower the heat and add the curry powder.
4. Put on the lid and let them cook for 6 min. Stir in the veggies and cook them until all the broth is absorbed.
5. Adjust the seasoning of your risotto then serve it warm.
6. Enjoy.

AUGUST'S
Quinoa Risotto

Prep Time: 15 mins
Total Time: 45 mins

Servings per Recipe: 4
Calories	636.7
Fat	30.9g
Cholesterol	41.6mg
Sodium	404.8mg
Carbohydrates	64.2g
Protein	26.8g

Ingredients

4 tbsp olive oil
1 onion, chopped
3 garlic cloves, minced
10 -15 button mushrooms, sliced
1 summer squash, sliced
2 C. quinoa
3 C. vegetable broth
1 C. milk

1 C. mozzarella cheese
1/2 C. parmesan cheese
salt and pepper

Directions

1. Place a large saucepan over medium heat. Heat in it the oil.
2. Cook in it the onion with garlic for 3 min. Stir in the mushrooms and cook them for 4 min.
3. Stir in the zucchini and cook them for 2 to 3 min. Stir in the quinoa and cook them for 1 min.
4. Stir in 1 C. of broth and cook them until the quinoa absorbs it.
5. Repeat the process with the remaining broth. Stir in the milk and cook the risotto until it becomes creamy.
6. Stir in the cheese with a pinch of salt and pepper. Heat it until it melts. Serve it warm.
7. Enjoy.

Gilroy
Garlic Risotto

🍲 Prep Time: 10 mins
🕐 Total Time: 40 mins

Servings per Recipe: 4
Calories	527.5
Fat	12.2g
Cholesterol	14.8mg
Sodium	772.5mg
Carbohydrates	90.7g
Protein	12.8g

Ingredients

2 C. Arborio rice
1 onion
2 vegetable bouillon cubes, dissolved in 1 ltr. hot water
1 bulb of garlic, minced
2 tbsp soy sauce
1 tsp chili flakes
1 tbsp basil

1 C. bell pepper
1/2 C. cheddar cheese
2/3 C. stewed tomatoes
2 tbsp olive oil
salt and pepper

Directions

1. Place a large saucepan over medium heat. Heat in it the oil. Cook in it the onion with garlic for 6 min.
2. Stir in the peppers and cook them for 3 min. Stir in the rice and cook them or 1 min.
3. Stir in a ladle of stock with the stewed tomatoes. Cook them while stirring the rice absorbs it.
4. Stir in the soy sauce, chili flakes, and basil.
5. Add the remaining stock gradually while stirring until the rice absorbs it all.
6. Stir into the cheese with a pinch of salt and pepper. Serve your risotto warm.
7. Enjoy.

5-INGREDIENT
Seafood Risotto

Prep Time: 5 mins
Total Time: 15 mins

Servings per Recipe: 2

Calories	342.5
Fat	22.7g
Cholesterol	281.4mg
Sodium	365.7mg
Carbohydrates	2.5g
Protein	30.9g

Ingredients

10.5 oz. approx. king prawns, defrosted
2 oz. butter
2 - 4 large garlic cloves, crushed
1 package of ready cooked mushroom

rice
salt and pepper

Directions

1. Place a skillet over medium heat. Heat in it the butter. Cook in it the garlic with prawns for 3 min.
2. Prepare the mushroom rice by following the instructions on the package.
3. Serve it warm with prawns.
4. Enjoy.

Risotto
with Scallops

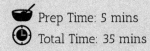 Prep Time: 5 mins

Total Time: 35 mins

Servings per Recipe: 4

Calories	537.7
Fat	11.4g
Cholesterol	27.2mg
Sodium	483.1mg
Carbohydrates	84.6g
Protein	21.5g

Ingredients

1 tbsp oil
cracked black pepper and sea salt
1 lb. scallops
5 1/2 C. of boiling vegetable stock
2 tbsp oil
2 C. Arborio rice

2 tsp lemon rind, grated
6 1/2 oz. baby spinach leaves
cracked black pepper and sea salt
parmesan cheese, shavings

Directions

1. Place a large saucepan over medium heat. Heat in it the oil.
2. Cook in it the rice for 1 min. Stir in the stock gradually while stirring until the rice absorbs it all.
3. Season it with a pinch of salt and pepper. Add the spinach with lemon rind.
4. Place a skillet over high heat. Season the scallops with a pinch of salt and pepper.
5. Sear them for 25 to 35 sec on each side. Spoon them over the risotto and serve them warm.
6. Enjoy.

SIMPLE
Pesto

Prep Time: 2 mins
Total Time: 12 mins

Servings per Recipe: 6
Calories   199 kcal
Fat   21.1 g
Carbohydrates   2g
Protein   1.7 g
Cholesterol   0 mg
Sodium   389 mg

Ingredients

1/4 C. almonds
3 cloves garlic
1 1/2 C. fresh basil leaves
1/2 C. olive oil

1 pinch ground nutmeg
salt and pepper to taste

Directions

1. Set your oven to 450 degrees F before doing anything else.
2. Arrange the almonds onto a cookie sheet and bake for about 10 minutes or till toasted slightly.
3. In a food processor, add the toasted almonds and the remaining ingredients till a rough paste forms.

Risotto
Chicken Dinner

🥣 Prep Time: 10 mins
🕐 Total Time: 30 mins

Servings per Recipe: 3
Calories	458.1
Fat	16.5g
Cholesterol	59.5mg
Sodium	735.1mg
Carbohydrates	47.6g
Protein	29.0g

Ingredients

2 tbsp olive oil
10.5 oz. skinless chicken breasts, sliced into strips
1 large bell pepper, julienned
1/4 large red onion, julienned
1 tbsp white pepper
1 tbsp minced garlic paste
1 tbsp dried oregano
1 tbsp chopped fresh basil
1 tsp soy sauce

2 C. cooked rice
1/4 C. sliced black olives
1 C. chicken gravy
grated parmesan cheese
dried parsley
fresh parsley sprig

Directions

1. Place a large pan over medium heat. Heat in it the oil.
2. Cook in it the chicken strips for 3 min. Stir in the bell pepper, onion, pepper, garlic, and oregano.
3. Cook them for 3 min. Stir in the basil, soy sauce, rice, and black olives. Cook them for another 3 min.
4. Stir in the gravy and cook them until they start boiling. Lower the heat and let them cook for 9 to 11 min.
5. Stir in the parsley flakes with parmesan cheese. Serve your risotto warm.
6. Enjoy.

ROASTED
Mozzarella Risotto

Prep Time: 30 mins
Total Time: 1 hr

Servings per Recipe: 10
Calories	386.5
Fat	18.8g
Cholesterol	94.0mg
Sodium	372.1mg
Carbohydrates	38.6g
Protein	16.4g

Ingredients

1.5 oz. butter
1 tbsp oil
1 large leek, sliced
1 garlic clove, crushed
2 C. Arborio rice
4 C. vegetable stock
1 C. water
1/2 C. cream
2 bunches asparagus, chopped
1.5 oz. baby spinach leaves

1 C. parmesan cheese, grated
2 tbsp parsley, chopped
2 eggs, lightly beaten
6.5 oz. baby bocconcini, drained
1/2 C. tasty cheese, grated

Directions

1. Place a large saucepan over medium heat. Heat in it the butter.
2. Cook in it the garlic with leek for 3 min. Stir in the rice and cook them for 2 min.
3. Stir in the water with cream and stock. Cook them until they start boiling.
4. Lower the heat and simmer it for 11 min.
5. Before you do anything, preheat the oven to 356 F.
6. Add the asparagus, spinach leaves, parmesan, and parsley.
7. Turn off the heat and add the eggs. Pour half of the mixture into a baking pan.
8. Top it with the bocconcini. Cover it with the remaining risotto. Top it with cheese.
9. Bake it for 26 min. Allow the risotto casserole to rest for 12 min. Serve it warm.
10. Enjoy.

Italian
Risotto

🍲 Prep Time: 15 mins
🕐 Total Time: 55 mins

Servings per Recipe: 4
Calories	760.1
Fat	17.3g
Cholesterol	15.2mg
Sodium	1017.3mg
Carbohydrates	128.1g
Protein	23.7g

Ingredients

4 C. vegetable broth
1 C. water
2 carrots, peeled and diced
12 stalks asparagus, trimmed and cut on the diagonal into lengths
2 bay leaves
2 tsp dried sage, divided
3 tbsp olive oil
1 large onion, chopped
1 lb. Arborio rice

1/2 C. limoncello, or chicken broth
2 C. fresh green peas
1/3 C. grated mozzarella cheese
1/4 C. grated parmesan cheese
salt and pepper

Directions

1. Place a large saucepan over medium heat. Stir in it the water with broth and heat them until they start boiling.
2. Stir in the carrots, asparagus, bay leaves, 1 tsp sage and salt and pepper.
3. Put on the lid and lower the heat. Let them cook for 12 min. Stain the veggies and place the broth aside.
4. Place a large pan over medium heat. Heat in it the oil. Cook in it the onion for 3 min.
5. Stir in the rice and cook them for 2 min. Stir in the limoncello and cook them for 1 min.
6. Stir 1 C. of broth and cook them until the rice absorbs it.
7. Repeat the process with the remaining broth until the rice absorbs all of it.
8. Turn off the heat and stir in the rest of the sage with veggies, green peas, and cheeses.
9. Cook them until the risotto becomes creamy. Serve it right away.
10. Enjoy.

25-MINUTE
Chicken Risotto

Prep Time: 10 mins
Total Time: 25 mins

Servings per Recipe: 4
Calories	342.9
Fat	5.6g
Cholesterol	79.4mg
Sodium	389.5mg
Carbohydrates	42.5g
Protein	28.4g

Ingredients

1/2 tbsp oil
1/2 onion, chopped
1 lb. ground chicken
1 (8 oz.) cans tomato sauce
1 C. long grain white rice, uncooked
1/4 C. parmesan cheese, grated

1/4-1/2 C. mozzarella cheese, shredded
salt and pepper

Directions

1. Prepare the rice by following the instructions on the package.
2. Place a large deep pan over medium heat. Heat in it the oil. Cook in it the onion for 3 min.
3. Stir in the meat with a pinch of salt and pepper. Cook them for 7 min. Discard the excess grease.
4. Stir in the tomato sauce and cook them for 2 min. Stir in the rice with cheeses.
5. Adjust the seasoning of your risotto then serve it warm.
6. Enjoy.

True
Country Risotto

Prep Time: 45 mins
Total Time: 45 mins

Servings per Recipe: 6
Calories	459.0
Fat	14.5g
Cholesterol	52.5mg
Sodium	1059.2mg
Carbohydrates	58.2g
Protein	14.6g

Ingredients

2 quarts chicken broth
18 large shrimp, peeled and deveined
2 tbsp olive oil
4 tbsp unsalted butter
1 large onion, peeled and diced
2 C. Arborio rice

1 C. vegetable broth
2 tbsp lemon zest
2 tbsp lemon juice
2 tbsp tarragon leaves, chopped

Directions

1. Place a large pot over medium heat. Heat in it the broth until it starts boiling.
2. Stir in the shrimp and cook them for 6 min. Drain it and place it aside.
3. Place a large saucepan over medium heat. Heat in it the oil with 2 tbsp of butter.
4. Cook in it the onion for 5 min. Stir in the vegetable broth and cook them until they start boiling.
5. Stir in the rice with 1 C. of boiling broth. Cook them while stirring until it is absorbed.
6. Repeat the process with the remaining broth until all of it is absorbed.
7. Add 1 tbsp of lemon juice, 1 tbsp of lemon zest, a pinch of salt and pepper. Cook them for 1 min.
8. Add the shrimp, tarragon and remaining 2 Tbsp butter. Serve your risotto warm.
9. Enjoy.

DIJON
Beef Risotto

Prep Time: 10 mins
Total Time: 25 mins

Servings per Recipe: 2

Calories	588.3
Fat	30.5g
Cholesterol	89.0mg
Sodium	557.7mg
Carbohydrates	47.4g
Protein	29.1g

Ingredients

8 oz. beef tenderloin steaks
1/4 C. kraft special collection sun-dried tomato vinaigrette dressing, Divided
3/4 C. zucchini, Chopped
1/4 C. carrot, Shredded
1/4 C. red pepper, Chopped

1 C. White Rice, Uncooked
3/4 C. chicken broth
1/2 C. milk
2 tbsp Grey Poupon Dijon Mustard

Directions

1. Place a large saucepan over medium heat. Heat in it 1 tbsp of dressing.
2. Cook in it the zucchini, carrot, and red pepper for 3 min.
3. Add the rice with broth, mustard, milk, a pinch of salt and pepper. Cook them until they start boiling.
4. Put on the lid and turn off the heat. Let it sit for 6 min.
5. Place a large pan over medium heat. Heat in it the rest of the dressing.
6. Cook in it the steaks for 5 to 6 min on each side. Serve them warm.
7. Enjoy.

Seattle
Vegetable Risotto

Prep Time: 10 mins
Total Time: 35 mins

Servings per Recipe: 6
Calories	777.8
Fat	36.0g
Cholesterol	94.1mg
Sodium	1688.3mg
Carbohydrates	89.9g
Protein	22.0g

Ingredients

10 C. chicken broth
1 1/2 lbs. small zucchini, chopped
10 oz. carrots, chopped
3/4 C. butter
3 C. Arborio rice
1/2 C. cream, scalded

3/4 C. grated parmesan cheese
2 tbsp minced parsley
1 tbsp minced basil

Directions

1. Place a large saucepan over medium heat. Heat in it the broth until it starts boiling.
2. Place a pot over medium heat. Stir in it the zucchini and carrots in ½ C. of butter. Cook them for 6 min.
3. Stir in 1 C. of stock. Cook them for 4 min while stirring until the rice absorbs it.
4. Repeat the process with the remaining broth until the rice absorbs all of it.
5. Once the time is up, add the rest of the butter with cream, a pinch of salt and pepper. Serve it warm.
6. Enjoy.

LATE OCTOBER
Pine Nut Risotto

Prep Time: 20 mins
Total Time: 1 hr

Servings per Recipe: 4
Calories	751.6
Fat	18.3g
Cholesterol	9.4mg
Sodium	138.5mg
Carbohydrates	129.3g
Protein	16.0g

Ingredients

2 tbsp olive oil
1 large onion, chopped
1 clove garlic, crushed
1 - 2 tbsp fresh sage
3 C. Arborio rice
2 C. fresh pumpkin, diced
1 3/4 pints boiling vegetable stock
1/3 C. pine nuts

1/3 C. shredded parmesan cheese
4 tbsp milk
1 pinch ground allspice
salt
ground black pepper

Directions

1. Place a large skillet over medium heat. Heat in it the oil.
2. Cook in it the sage with onion and sage for 6 min. Stir in the pumpkin with rice.
3. Cook them for 2 min. Stir 1/4 pint of stock. Cook them until the rice absorbs it while stirring.
4. Repeat the process with the remaining stock until the risotto becomes creamy.
5. Get a food processor: Combine in it the pine nuts, cheese, milk, and allspice. Blend them smooth.
6. Add it to the risotto with a pinch of salt and pepper. Cook them for 3 min then serve it warm.
7. Enjoy.

Oyster Mushroom and Barley Risotto (Brown Basmati Risotto)

Prep Time: 10 mins
Total Time: 1 hr 10 mins

Servings per Recipe: 4

Calories	194.3
Fat	3.8g
Cholesterol	5.5mg
Sodium	126.1mg
Carbohydrates	33.5g
Protein	9.5g

Ingredients

6 C. water
2/3 brown basmati rice
2/3 C. pearl barley
1 tsp olive oil
1 lb. oyster mushroom, sliced
1/2 C. vegetable broth

1/4 C. grated parmesan cheese
1/4 tsp ground pepper

Directions

1. Place a pot over medium heat. Heat in it the water until it starts boiling.
2. Stir in it the barley with rice and a pinch of salt. Bring them to a boil.
3. Lower the heat and let them cook for 46 min while stirring often.
4. Place a large skillet over medium heat. Heat in it the oil.
5. Cook in it the mushrooms for 9 min. Drain the rice and barley then add them to the pan.
6. Cook them for 2 min. Stir in the cheese with broth. Cook them until the risotto becomes creamy.
7. Adjust its seasoning then serve it warm.
8. Enjoy.

OVEN ROASTED
Risotto

🍲 Prep Time: 20 mins

🕐 Total Time: 1 hr 10 mins

Servings per Recipe: 6	
Calories	391.6
Fat	23.9g
Cholesterol	42.3mg
Sodium	620.4mg
Carbohydrates	37.2g
Protein	8.3g

Ingredients

4 tbsp butter
1 onion, chopped
1 tbsp minced garlic
2 celery ribs, diced
1 small green bell pepper, seeded and chopped
1 (10 oz.) can cream of mushroom soup, undiluted
5 oz. milk
1 (10 oz.) cans sliced mushrooms, well drained, sliced and sautéed
1/2 C. mayonnaise
1/2 C. sour cream
black pepper
1/2 tsp garlic powder
2 1/2 C. cold cooked rice
1/3 C. grated parmesan cheese

Directions

1. Before you do anything, preheat the oven to 350 F.
2. Grease a baking dish with some butter. Place it aside.
3. Place a large pan over medium heat. Heat in it the butter. Cook in it the onion with bell pepper and celery for 6 min.
4. Stir in the garlic and cook them for 3 min. Drain the mixture and place it in a large bowl.
5. Stir the soup, milk, drained canned mushrooms mayonnaise, sour cream, black pepper, garlic powder and cooked cold rice.
6. Season them with a pinch of salt and pepper. Combine them well. Spoon the mixture into the greased casserole.
7. Top it with cheese then bake it for 36 to 46 min. Serve it warm.
8. Enjoy.

Oyster Mushroom
and Barley Risotto (Brown Basmati Risotto)

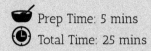 Prep Time: 5 mins

Total Time: 25 mins

Servings per Recipe: 4

Calories	397.0
Fat	17.9g
Cholesterol	47.0mg
Sodium	767.9mg
Carbohydrates	44.8g
Protein	13.5g

Ingredients

1 medium onion, diced
4 tbsp butter
1 lemon, zest, and juice
1 C. Arborio rice
2 C. chicken broth
2 C. water

3/4 C. grated parmesan cheese
2 tbsp chopped parsley
additional parmesan cheese

Directions

1. Place a large saucepan over medium heat. Heat in it the butter.
2. Cook in it the lemon zest with onion for 3 min. Stir in the rice and cook them for 1 min.
3. Lower the heat and stir in 1/2 C. of broth with 2 tbsp of lemon juice.
4. Let them cook until the risotto becomes thick.
5. Stir in 1/2 C. of broth and simmer it again until it becomes thick.
6. Repeat the process with the remaining broth. When the rice is done, stir in the cheese with parsley.
7. Adjust the seasoning of your risotto then serve it warm.
8. Enjoy.

PITTSBURGH STYLE
Risotto

Prep Time: 10 mins
Total Time: 40 mins

Servings per Recipe: 4
Calories	599.8
Fat	17.4g
Cholesterol	47.1mg
Sodium	912.3mg
Carbohydrates	78.8g
Protein	24.9g

Ingredients

2 tbsp butter
2 1/2 C. fresh mushrooms, sliced
1 - 2 pieces skinless chicken breast, chopped
5 1/2 C. chicken stock, heated
1 1/2 C. Arborio rice
1/2 C. broth
1 large chopped onion

4 garlic cloves, crushed
1 C. of grated parmesan cheese
1/4 C. cream
2 tbsp of chopped parsley
oil
salt & pepper

Directions

1. Place a soup stew pot over medium heat. Heat in it the oil.
2. Cook in it the mushrooms with chicken for 5 min. Drain them and place them aside.
3. Stir the butter with onion and garlic in the same pot. Cook them for 3 min.
4. Stir in the rice and cook them for 2 min. Stir in the broth with a pinch of salt and pepper.
5. Cook them until the rice absorbs the broth. Stir in 1/2 C. of chicken stock. Simmer the risotto until it becomes thick.
6. Repeat the process with the remaining broth until the risotto is done.
7. Stir the mushroom and rice back to the pot. Cook them for 2 min.
8. Stir in 1/2 C. of cheese with parsley, cream, a pinch of salt and pepper.
9. Garnish your risotto with the remaining cheese then serve it hot.
10. Enjoy.

Fathia's
Favorite Risotto

🥣 Prep Time: 15 mins
🕐 Total Time: 1 hr

Servings per Recipe: 4
Calories	365.0
Fat	9.6g
Cholesterol	16.4mg
Sodium	521.3mg
Carbohydrates	53.9g
Protein	15.4g

Ingredients

1 tbsp olive oil
1 C. chopped onion
1 C. Arborio rice
4 oz. fresh spinach leaves
3 C. chicken stock
1 dash salt

1 dash allspice
1/2 C. grated parmesan cheese
1 1/2 C. asparagus, sliced

Directions

1. Before you do anything, preheat the oven to 400 F.
2. Place an ovenproof over medium heat. Heat in it the oil.
3. Cook in it the onion for 3 min. Stir in the rice and cook them for 2 min.
4. Add the spinach, with 2 C. of stock, and salt. Let them cook for 8 min.
5. Add 1/4 C. of cheese. Stir them well. Place the pot in the oven.
6. Let it cook for 16 min. Add the asparagus with 1/4 C. of cheese, and 1/2 C. of stock.
7. Cook it for an extra 16 min. Serve your risotto hot.
8. Enjoy.

ROMANO
Mushroom

Prep Time: 10 mins
Total Time: 35 mins

Servings per Recipe: 6

Calories	301.2
Fat	15.2g
Cholesterol	27.7mg
Sodium	535.2mg
Carbohydrates	31.9g
Protein	9.7g

Ingredients

1 lb. mushroom, sliced
4 tbsp butter
2 tbsp olive oil
1 onion, chopped
2 garlic cloves, minced
1 C. Arborio rice
3 C. hot chicken stock
1 C. hot water

1/2 C. romano cheese, shredded
1/2 C. parsley, chopped
salt and pepper

Directions

1. Place a large pan over medium heat. Heat in it the butter.
2. Cook in it the mushrooms with a pinch of salt and pepper for 3 min.
3. Drain it and place it aside.
4. Heat the oil in the same pan. Cook in it the onion with garlic for 3 to 4 min.
5. Add the rice and cook them for 2 min. Add 1 C. of broth and simmer it until it rice absorbs it while stirring from time to time.
6. Repeat the process with the remaining broth and water until the rice is done.
7. Fold the mushrooms with cheese, parsley, a pinch of salt and pepper into the risotto.
8. Serve your risotto hot.
9. Enjoy.

Cream
of Risotto

Prep Time: 10 mins
Total Time: 40 mins

Servings per Recipe: 6
Calories	282.1
Fat	10.9g
Cholesterol	22.5mg
Sodium	584.0mg
Carbohydrates	36.4g
Protein	9.5g

Ingredients

2 tbsp butter
1/3 C. onion, chopped
1 C. uncooked white Arborio rice
1 (10 3/4 oz.) can cream of mushroom soup, undiluted
1 1/2 C. chicken stock

1 C. milk
1/3 C. grated parmesan cheese
1/4 tsp fresh ground black pepper
1 (10 oz.) cans sliced mushrooms, well drained

Directions

1. Before you do anything, preheat the oven to 400 F.
2. Get a mixing bowl: Stir in it the stock with milk, cheese, a pinch of salt and pepper.
3. Place an ovenproof pot over medium heat. Heat in it the butter.
4. Cook in it the onion for 5 min. Stir in the rice and cook them for 1 min.
5. Stir in the mushroom soup with mushrooms, and stock mixture.
6. Put on the lid and place the pot in the oven for 26 min.
7. Once the time is up, stir the risotto and bake it for an extra 12 min.
8. Adjust the seasoning of the risotto then let it rest for 6 min. Serve it warm.
9. Enjoy.

NEW YORK STYLE
Risotto

Prep Time: 5 mins
Total Time: 40 mins

Servings per Recipe: 4

Calories	643.4
Fat	19.5g
Cholesterol	42.2mg
Sodium	736.2mg
Carbohydrates	94.1g
Protein	20.0g

Ingredients

2 tbsp butter
1 tbsp olive oil
1 onion, chopped
5 1/2 C. of hot chicken stock
2 C. Arborio rice
3 tsp lemon rind, grated
1/2 C. parmesan cheese, grated
2 tbsp butter

sea salt
cracked black pepper

Directions

1. Place a large saucepan over medium heat. Heat in it the butter with oil.
2. Cook in it the onion for 7 min. Stir in the lemon rind with rice. Cook them for 2 min while stirring.
3. Add the hot stock gradually while stirring all the time.
4. Let the risotto cook for 25 to 28 min until it is done.
5. Stir in the cheese with butter, a pinch of salt and pepper. Serve it hot.
6. Enjoy

Spinach
Risotto

🥣 Prep Time: 20 mins
🕐 Total Time: 45 mins

Servings per Recipe: 4
Calories   515.7
Fat   28.1g
Cholesterol   0.0mg
Sodium   146.1mg
Carbohydrates   59.0g
Protein   9.6g

Ingredients

1 1/2lbs.s spinach, cleaned, stemmed, torn
1/2 C. olive oil
1 C. chopped spring onion, white and green
1 small onion, chopped
1 leek, chopped
1 1/4 C. rice, short-grain
1/4 C. lemon juice

2 tbsp minced dill
3 C. water
salt
fresh ground black pepper
1 tbsp tomato paste

Directions

1. Place a deep skillet over medium heat. Heat in it the oil. Cook in it the leek with onion for 3 min.
2. Stir in the rice and cook them for 4 min.
3. Stir in the water with dill, lemon juice, spring onion, tomato paste, a pinch of salt and pepper.
4. Cook the risotto until it starts boiling. Lower the heat and let it cook for 11 min.
5. Once the time is up, stir in the spinach and put on the lid. Let them cook for 6 min.
6. Turn off the heat and put on the lid. Let the risotto cook for 32 min.
7. Serve it with toppings of your choice.
8. Enjoy.

RISOTTO
101

Prep Time: 15 mins
Total Time: 40 mins

Servings per Recipe: 4	
Calories	578.6
Fat	23.6g
Cholesterol	45.2mg
Sodium	366.3mg
Carbohydrates	77.2g
Protein	13.5g

Ingredients

1 C. leek, sliced
1 C. cremini mushroom, sliced
2 tbsp olive oil
2 - 3 garlic cloves, minced
4 tbsp butter
1 small yellow onion, chopped
1 3/4 C. Arborio rice
5 C. fresh vegetable stock
1 lemon, juice and zest

2/3 C. parmesan cheese
2 tbsp chives, minced
1/4 C. Italian parsley, chopped
salt
fresh ground black pepper
lemon wedge
fresh Italian parsley

Directions

1. Place a large skillet over medium heat. Heat in it the oil.
2. Cook in it the leeks with mushrooms for 6 min.
3. Stir in the garlic and cook them for 1 min. Drain the veggies mixture and place it aside.
4. Heat 2 tbsp of butter in the same skillet. cook in it the onion for 6 min.
5. Add the rice and cook them for 2 min. Stir in a splash of stock and cook them until the rice absorbs it.
6. Add the remaining stock gradually until the risotto becomes creamy.
7. Add the cooked leeks and mushroom.
8. Adjust the seasoning of your risotto then garnish it with cheese. Serve it warm.
9. Enjoy.

Risotto
Persian

Prep Time: 10 mins
Total Time: 50 mins

Servings per Recipe: 4
Calories	561.1
Fat	25.5g
Cholesterol	67.8mg
Sodium	1652.2mg
Carbohydrates	63.1g
Protein	18.4g

Ingredients

5 C. of hot beef stock
1 pinch saffron
6 tbsp butter
1 onion, chopped
1 1/2 C. Arborio rice

1 C. grated parmesan cheese
salt and pepper

Directions

1. Get a small mixing bowl: Stir in it the saffron with a splash of hot stock. Let it sit for few minutes.
2. Place a large deep pan over medium heat. Heat in it 4 tbsp of butter.
3. Cook in it the onion for 4 min. Stir in the rice and cook them for 1 min.
4. Stir in the saffron mixture with a pinch of salt and pepper. Add the remaining stock gradually while stirring.
5. Lower the heat and put on the lid. Cook the risotto for 22 to 26 min until it becomes creamy while stirring it often.
6. Fold the remaining butter and cheese into the risotto. Serve it immediately.
7. Enjoy.

AFRICAN
Quinoa "Risotto"

Prep Time: 10 mins
Total Time: 25 mins

Servings per Recipe: 4	
Calories	281.8
Fat	8.8g
Cholesterol	0.0mg
Sodium	27.2mg
Carbohydrates	42.3g
Protein	9.5g

Ingredients

1 tbsp olive oil
1/2 C. red onion, chopped
1/4 C. green onion, chopped
2 garlic cloves, peeled and minced
1/2 C. quinoa, rinsed and drained
1/2 C. Israeli couscous
1 C. orange juice
1 1/8 C. low sodium chicken broth
1/2 tsp ground ginger

1 tsp ground cumin
1/4 C. slivered almonds, toasted
salt and pepper

Directions

1. Place a large pan over medium heat. Heat in it the oil.
2. Cook in it the onion for 3 min. Stir in the green onion with garlic. Cook them for 2 min.
3. Add the quinoa with couscous, orange juice, broth, ginger, cumin, almonds, a pinch of salt and pepper.
4. Cook them until they start boiling. Lower the heat and put on the lid. Cook them for 16 min.
5. Once the time is up, remove the lid and fold the almonds into the risotto.
6. Let it cook until it becomes creamy for few minutes.
7. Serve your risotto warm right away.
8. Enjoy.

Nana's
Asiago "Risotto"

🥣 Prep Time: 10 mins
🕐 Total Time: 30 mins

Servings per Recipe: 6
Calories	349.3
Fat	6.6g
Cholesterol	13.3mg
Sodium	334.6mg
Carbohydrates	57.6g
Protein	13.3g

Ingredients

1 (1 lb.) box orzo pasta
2 C. chicken broth
1 tbsp minced garlic
1 oz. shredded Parmigiano
1 oz. shredded asiago cheese

2 tbsp unsalted butter
salt and pepper

Directions

1. Prepare the risotto by following the instructions on the package. Drain it.
2. Place a large deep pan over medium heat. Stir in it the garlic with broth. Cook it until the broth evaporates.
3. Add the butter with cheese, a pinch of salt and pepper. Serve your risotto right away.
4. Enjoy.

MEDITERRANEAN
Risotto Greek Style

Prep Time: 10 mins
Total Time: 30 mins

Servings per Recipe: 5
Calories	415.8
Fat	22.1g
Cholesterol	0.0mg
Sodium	53.4mg
Carbohydrates	50.8g
Protein	4.6g

Ingredients

6 large leeks, cleaned and sliced
1 large red onion, minced
1/2 C. boiling water
1/2-3/4 C. olive oil
1 tbsp tomato paste
1 C. Arborio rice
4 1/2 C. boiling water
3 tbsp minced fresh dill
1/2 lemon, juice and zest

Toppings
- grated parmesan cheese
- cracked black pepper

Directions

1. Place a pot over medium heat. Heat in it the oil. Cook in it the leeks with onion for 4 min.
2. Stir in 1/2 C. of water with tomato paste. Cook them until they start simmering.
3. Put on the lid and let them cook for 22 min while stirring often.
4. Stir in the rice and cook them until they start boiling. Put on the lid and lower the heat.
5. Cook the risotto for 16 min while stirring often until it becomes creamy.
6. Fold the dill with lemon juice and zest into the risotto.
7. Garnish it with some parmesan cheese then serve it warm.
8. Enjoy.

Simple
French Style Risotto

Prep Time: 10 mins
Total Time: 45 mins

Servings per Recipe: 4
Calories   572.7
Fat   26.3g
Cholesterol   28.9mg
Sodium   1070.2mg
Carbohydrates   66.6g
Protein   18.7g

Ingredients

1 bunch beet
5 C. unsalted chicken stock
1 tsp sea salt
2 tbsp olive oil
1 tbsp unsalted butter

2 - 3 shallots
1 1/2 C. Arborio rice
4 - 5 oz. gorgonzola
1/3 C. walnuts

Directions

1. Bring a large pot of water to a boil. Cook in it the beets until they become soft.
2. Drain them and place them aside to cool down. Peel them and cut them into 3/4 inch dices.
3. Place a saucepan over medium heat. Heat in it 5 C. of chicken broth. Bring them to a boil.
4. Place a large skillet over medium heat. Heat in it 2 tbsp of olive oil with 1 tbsp of butter.
5. Cook in it the shallots for 9 min. Stir in 1 1/2 C. of rice. cook them for 4 min while stirring it.
6. Stir in 1/2 C. of hot stock and cook it until the rice absorbs it.
7. Stir in the remaining stock gradually while stirring.
8. Put on the lid and let the risotto cook for 15 to 20 min until it becomes creamy.
9. Stir in the beets with gorgonzola cheese and walnuts. Serve your risotto immediately.
10. Enjoy.

HOW TO MAKE
a Risotto

🥣 Prep Time: 10 mins
🕐 Total Time: 35 mins

Servings per Recipe: 2
Calories   692.6
Fat   10.0g
Cholesterol   8.9mg
Sodium   185.9mg
Carbohydrates   135.7g
Protein   12.8g

Ingredients

5 C. vegetable stock
4 carrots, cut into matchsticks
1 onion, small, diced
1 tbsp olive oil
1 1/2 C. Arborio rice
1 tsp dried dill

1 lemon, juice
20 g feta, crumbled, grated
2 tbsp parsley, chopped

Directions

1. Place a large saucepan over medium heat. Heat in it the stock until it starts boiling.
2. Stir in the carrots. Lower the heat and let them cook.
3. Place a large saucepan over medium heat. Heat in it the oil. Cook in it the onion for 3 min.
4. Stir in the rice and cook them for 1 min. Stir in the dill with C. of the carrot stock mixture while stirring.
5. Add the remaining stock while stirring until the rice is done for 16 to 22 min.
6. Once the time is up, add the lemon juice with feta and parsley.
7. Adjust the seasoning of your risotto then serve it warm.
8. Enjoy.

Tallahassee
Seafood Risotto

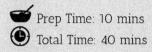 Prep Time: 10 mins

Total Time: 40 mins

Servings per Recipe: 4
Calories	370.0
Fat	16.0g
Cholesterol	101.9mg
Sodium	634.9mg
Carbohydrates	27.5g
Protein	27.4g

Ingredients

4 tbsp butter
14 oz. skinless firm white fish fillets, cut
5 C. of boiling a fish stock
1 onion, chopped
1 garlic clove, crushed
1 tsp ground turmeric
12 oz. risotto rice
2 tbsp lemon juice

1 tbsp chopped fresh parsley
1 tbsp snipped chives
1 tbsp chopped dill
sliced lemons

Directions

1. Place a large skillet over medium heat. Heat in it half of the butter.
2. Fry in it the fish fillets for 3 to 4 min on each side. Drain them and place them aside.
3. Heat the remaining butter in the same pan. Cook in it the onion with garlic for 4 min.
4. Stir in the turmeric with rice and cook them for 1 min.
5. Stir in 1/2 C. of stock while stirring until the rice absorbs it all.
6. Repeat the process with the remaining boiling stock until the rice becomes creamy.
7. Add the chives with dill, lemon juice, and parsley.
8. Adjust the seasoning of your risotto then stir into it the fish. Serve it hot.
9. Enjoy.

RISOTTO
Brasileiro

Prep Time: 20 mins
Total Time: 1 hr 20 mins

Servings per Recipe: 4

Calories	541.8
Fat	30.4g
Cholesterol	122.2mg
Sodium	1521.7mg
Carbohydrates	28.2g
Protein	36.2g

Ingredients

9 oz. cherry tomatoes
1 red onion, chopped
2 garlic cloves, chopped
2 tbsp olive oil
10 oz. risotto rice
4 chicken thigh fillets, halved
7 oz. beef sausage, sliced
2 tsp fresh rosemary, chopped
4 1/4 C. hot chicken broth

1 pinch saffron strand
8 large raw shrimp
salt and black pepper

Directions

1. Before you do anything, preheat the oven to 425 F.
2. Toss in it the cherry tomatoes with red onion, olive oil, and garlic.
3. Cook them in the oven for 22 min.
4. Once the time is up, add the rice, chicken, sausage rosemary, chicken broth, saffron and some salt and pepper.
5. Stir them well. Bake the risotto for 22 min. Stir in the shrimp then bake it for 9 to 11 min.
6. Adjust the seasoning of your risotto then serve it warm.
7. Enjoy.

Caprese
Risotto

Prep Time: 30 mins
Total Time: 1 hr

Servings per Recipe: 10
Calories	229.1
Fat	5.6g
Cholesterol	17.6mg
Sodium	261.6mg
Carbohydrates	34.3g
Protein	9.3g

Ingredients

5 1/2 C. vegetable stock
1/3 C. sun-dried tomato, drained and chopped
1 onion, chopped
2 C. Arborio rice

1 C. mozzarella cheese, shredded
1 C. grated parmesan cheese
1/4 C. basil, chopped
salt and pepper

Directions

1. Place a large saucepan over medium heat. Heat in it the stock until it starts boiling.
2. Place a large pan over medium heat. Heat in it 2 tbsp of the reserved tomato oil.
3. Cook in it the onion for 5 min. Stir in the rice and cook them for 2 min.
4. Stir in the boiling stock one ladle at a time until the rice absorbs all of it and it becomes creamy.
5. Stir in the cheese with sun-dried tomatoes, remaining tomato oil, basil, a pinch of salt and pepper.
6. Serve your risotto immediately.
7. Enjoy.

NO RICE
Risotto

Prep Time: 14 mins
Total Time: 1 hr

Servings per Recipe: 4
Calories	84.9
Fat	4.6g
Cholesterol	0.0mg
Sodium	294.1mg
Carbohydrates	10.7g
Protein	1.5g

Ingredients

4 - 6 tsp olive oil
1 1/2 inches cinnamon sticks
1 medium onion, chopped
1/2 lb. pumpkin, peeled and diced
1/2 C. coarse cut Bulgar wheat

1/2 tsp salt
3/4 C. water

Directions

1. Place a pot over high heat. Heat in it the oil. Cook in it the cinnamon stick for 5 sec.
2. Stir in the onion and cook them for 3 min. Stir in the bulgur with pumpkin and salt. Cook them for 2 min.
3. Stir in the broth and cook them until they start boiling. Put on the lid and lower the heat.
4. Let the risotto cook for 28 to 30 min until it becomes creamy.
5. Adjust the seasoning of your risotto then serve it immediately.
6. Enjoy.

Picnic
Risotto

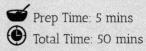 Prep Time: 5 mins

Total Time: 50 mins

Servings per Recipe: 6
Calories	409.2
Fat	16.5g
Cholesterol	28.9mg
Sodium	1240.0mg
Carbohydrates	44.0g
Protein	19.2g

Ingredients

1 1/2 C. Arborio rice
1 tbsp olive oil
3 (14 oz.) can chicken broth, reduced sodium
1/2 lb. Italian chicken sausage, casings removed, optional
1/2 lb. baby Bella mushroom, quartered

1/4 onion, minced
herbs
black pepper
1/2 C. parmesan cheese, grated

Directions

1. Place a pot over medium heat. Heat in it the broth until it starts boiling.
2. Place a large saucepan over medium heat. Heat in it the oil. Cook in it the onion with sausage for 4 min.
3. Stir in the mushrooms and cook them for 3 min. Add the rice and cook them for 1 min.
4. Stir in the broth gradually one broth at a time while stirring until the risotto is done and becomes creamy.
5. Turn off the heat and fold the cheese into the risotto. Serve it warm.
6. Enjoy.

MINTY
Garden Risotto

Prep Time: 15 mins
Total Time: 45 mins

Servings per Recipe: 6

Calories	323.2
Fat	11.3g
Cholesterol	22.6mg
Sodium	217.3mg
Carbohydrates	45.9g
Protein	10.2g

Ingredients

1 lb. asparagus, tough ends removed
and sliced into disks
1 tbsp extra virgin olive oil
3 tbsp butter, divided
2 C. low sodium chicken broth
2 C. water
1 small onion, chopped
1 1/2 C. Arborio rice
1/2 C. vegetable broth

1/2 C. parmesan cheese, grated
1/4 C. of fresh mint, chopped
1 lemon, juice and zest
salt
pepper

Directions

1. Place a large saucepan over medium heat. Stir in it the stock with water. Bring them to simmer.
2. Place a pot over medium heat. Heat in it the oil with 1 tbsp of butter.
3. Cook in it the onion for 3 min. Stir in the rice and cook them for 1 min.
4. Add the vegetable broth and cook them until it evaporates.
5. Add the hot stock and water mix gradually 1/2 C. at a time while stirring until the rice is done and creamy.
6. Turn off the heat and add the cheese with remaining butter, mint, lemon zest and juice.
7. Adjust the seasoning of your risotto then serve it warm.
8. Enjoy.

Wisconsin
Country Risotto

🥣 Prep Time: 10 mins
🕐 Total Time: 1 hr

Servings per Recipe: 2

Calories	242.1
Fat	7.2g
Cholesterol	6.6mg
Sodium	124.0mg
Carbohydrates	39.2g
Protein	7.4g

Ingredients

2 1/2 C. low sodium vegetable broth
2 tsp olive oil
1/2 C. onion, chopped
1 C. butternut squash, diced
1/3 C. pearl barley
1 tbsp fresh sage, chopped
3 tbsp parmesan cheese

2 tbsp fresh parsley, chopped
salt and pepper

Directions

1. Place a small pan over medium heat. Heat in it the broth until it starts boiling.
2. Place a large saucepan over medium heat. Heat in it the oil.
3. Cook in it the onion for 3 min. Stir in the squash and cook them for 4 min.
4. Stir in the barley and cook them for 1 min.
5. Stir 1/2 C. of the boiling broth with sage, a pinch of salt and pepper.
6. Let them cook while stirring for 6 min. Stir in the rest of the broth gradually.
7. Let the risotto cook while stirring it often for 36 to 42 min until it becomes creamy.
8. Once the time is up, turn off the heat and add the parsley with cheese.
9. Adjust the seasoning of your risotto then serve it hot.
10. Enjoy.

NEW HAMPSHIRE
Restaurant Risotto

Prep Time: 30 mins
Total Time: 1 hr 5 mins

Servings per Recipe: 4
Calories	572.5
Fat	18.5g
Cholesterol	111.9mg
Sodium	1509.7mg
Carbohydrates	70.7g
Protein	29.7g

Ingredients

2 tbsp butter
2 tbsp olive oil
2 garlic cloves, minced
8 oz. medium shrimp, shelled, deveined and chopped
8 oz. bay scallops, chopped
1/4 C. minced parsley
1 large yellow onion, chopped
1 1/2 C. long grain white rice
2 C. chicken broth
1 C. water
1/2 tsp salt
1/4 tsp black pepper
2 stalks celery, chopped
2 medium carrots, peeled and chopped
1 large tomatoes, cored, peeled and chopped
8 oz. asparagus spears
1/2 C. grated parmesan cheese

Directions

1. Place a large pot over medium heat. Heat in it the oil and butter.
2. Cook in it the garlic for 30 sec. Stir in the parsley with scallops and shrimp.
3. Cook them for 4 min while stirring. Drain and place them aside.
4. Combine the broth with water, rice, and 1/8 tsp of salt and pepper in the same pot.
5. Cook them until they start simmering. Lower the heat and put on the lid. Cook them for 11 min.
6. Stir in the carrots with tomato and celery. Put on the lid and cook them for 6 min.
7. Arrange asparagus on top of them and let them cook for another 6 min until the rice is done.
8. Once the time is up, fold the shrimp mixture into the pot.
9. Adjust the seasoning of your risotto then serve it hot.
10. Enjoy.

Mediterranean
Lentil Risotto

Prep Time: 10 mins
Total Time: 50 mins

Servings per Recipe: 10
Calories	145.2
Fat	5.8g
Cholesterol	13.1mg
Sodium	3.5mg
Carbohydrates	20.0g
Protein	3.5g

Ingredients

1 C. basmati rice, rinsed, soaked and drained
1 C. assorted lentils, rinsed, soaked and drained.
1/2 tsp turmeric powder
4 -6 tbsp ghee
1 cinnamon stick
4 bay leaves
4 cloves
6 cardamom pods
3 tsp cumin seeds
1 onion, chopped
4 garlic cloves
salt
lemon juice
cilantro

Directions

1. Place a large pot over medium heat. Combine in it the rice with lentils. Cover them with water.
2. Cook them until they start boiling. Lower the heat and stir in the turmeric with salt.
3. Put on the lid and let them cook for 32 min until they are done.
4. Place a saucepan over medium heat. Melt in it the ghee.
5. Cook in it the cinnamon stick, bay leaves, cloves, cardamom and cumin seeds for 1 min.
6. Stir in the garlic with the onion and cook them for 3 min. Spoon the mixture into the rice and lentil mix.
7. Once the time is up, stir in the lemon juice. Adjust the seasoning of your risotto then serve it warm.
8. Enjoy.

FULL VEGGIE
Risotto

Prep Time: 15 mins
Total Time: 50 mins

Servings per Recipe: 4

Calories	408.2
Fat	17.5g
Cholesterol	36.8mg
Sodium	327.1mg
Carbohydrates	47.8g
Protein	15.2g

Ingredients

2 C. sliced fresh mushrooms
1 medium onion, chopped
2 garlic cloves, minced
2 tbsp olive oil
1 C. Arborio rice
3 C. vegetable broth
3/4 C. bite-size asparagus, pieces
1 medium tomatoes, seeded and diced
1/4 C. shredded carrot

1 C. shredded Fontina cheese
1/4 C. grated parmesan cheese
3 tbsp snipped basil
tomatoes, slices

Directions

1. Place a pot over medium heat. Heat in it the oil.
2. Cook in it the mushroom with garlic and oil for 4 min.
3. Add the rice and cook them for 4 min. Stir in 1 C. of broth stir them until the rice absorbs it.
4. Repeat the process with the remaining broth until 1/2 C. is left.
5. Add the carrot with tomato and remaining broth. Let them cook until the rice becomes creamy.
6. Once the time is up, add the cheese with basil, a pinch of salt and pepper.
7. Serve your risotto warm.
8. Enjoy.

South American
Kidney Beans Risotto

🥣 Prep Time: 20 mins
🕐 Total Time: 50 mins

Servings per Recipe: 4
Calories	423.5
Fat	11.6g
Cholesterol	11.0mg
Sodium	537.7mg
Carbohydrates	64.1g
Protein	15.9g

Ingredients

3 C. vegetable broth
2 C. sliced mushrooms
1 medium onion, chopped
2 garlic cloves, minced
2 tbsp olive oil
1 C. Arborio rice
1 C. chopped zucchini
1 C. chopped carrot
1/2 C. shredded parmesan cheese

1 (15 oz.) cans white kidney beans, rinsed and drained
2 tbsp snipped fresh flat-leaf Italian parsley
shredded parmesan cheese

Directions

1. Place a saucepan over medium heat. Heat in it the broth until it starts boiling.
2. Place a pot over medium heat. Heat in it the oil. Cook in it the onion with garlic and mushroom for 6 min.
3. Stir in the rice and cook them for 6 min. Stir in 1 C. of broth while stirring all the time.
4. Let it cook until the rice absorbs it. Stir in 1/2 C. of broth with carrots, zucchini, a pinch of salt and pepper.
5. Cook them until the rice absorbs all the broth while stirring all the time.
6. Stir in the remaining broth gradually until the rice absorbs it all and becomes creamy.
7. Add the cheese with beans and stir them for 2 min.
8. Garnish your risotto with some parsley then serve it warm.
9. Enjoy.

DOWNSTATE
Risotto

Prep Time: 15 mins
Total Time: 45 mins

Servings per Recipe: 6
Calories	338.2
Fat	11.7g
Cholesterol	17.5mg
Sodium	200.6mg
Carbohydrates	48.5g
Protein	10.8g

Ingredients

1 1/4 lbs. asparagus, trimmed
2 C. of hot reduced-sodium chicken broth
2 tbsp olive oil
1 1/2 C. chopped onions
1 1/2 C. Arborio rice

1/4 C. grated parmesan cheese
2 tbsp butter
1/4 C. shaved parmesan cheese

Directions

1. Place a large saucepan over medium heat. Heat in it 5 C. of salted water until it starts boiling.
2. Stir in the asparagus and cook it for 5 min. Drain it and plunge it in ice water. Drain it again.
3. Reserve 3 1/2 C. of the cooking liquid. Trim and slice the asparagus into 1/4 inch pieces.
4. Place a pot over high heat. Heat in it the asparagus liquid with broth until they start boiling.
5. Place a large saucepan over medium heat. Heat in it the oil.
6. Cook in it the onion for 4 min. Stir in the rice and cook them for 2 to 3 min.
7. Stir in 2/3 C. of hot stock and asparagus liquid mixture. Cook them until the rice absorbs it while stirring often.
8. Repeat the process with the remaining broth mixture.
9. Cook the risotto until the rice is done and creamy.
10. Stir in the asparagus with cheese, butter, a pinch of salt and pepper.
11. Serve your risotto hot with some extra cheese for garnish.
12. Enjoy.

Easy
Peasey Risotto

Prep Time: 30 mins
Total Time: 30 mins

Servings per Recipe: 4
Calories	592.9
Fat	27.9g
Cholesterol	73.9mg
Sodium	820.7mg
Carbohydrates	65.8g
Protein	18.6g

Ingredients

6 C. of boiling chicken stock
3.5 oz. butter, unsalted
2 medium onions, chopped
1 garlic clove, crushed
8 oz. Arborio rice

4 oz. frozen peas
2 oz. parmesan cheese, grated

Directions

1. Place a large deep pan over medium heat. Heat in it the butter.
2. Cook in it the onion with garlic for 6 min. Stir in the rice and cook them for 1 min.
3. Stir in the boiling stock gradually while stirring all the time until the rice absorbs it and becomes creamy.
4. Stir in the peas and cook them for 4 min. Add the cheese with a pinch of salt and pepper.
5. Serve your risotto hot.
6. Enjoy.

SAVORY
Cinnamon Risotto

Prep Time: 10 mins
Total Time: 1 hr 45 mins

Servings per Recipe: 2

Calories	347.3
Fat	15.6g
Cholesterol	0.0mg
Sodium	540.5mg
Carbohydrates	45.8g
Protein	7.2g

Ingredients

3/8 C. brown rice, risotto
1 1/4 C. chicken broth
4 small carrots, chopped
1 shallot, chopped
1/8 C. raisins

1/3 stick cinnamon
2 tbsp olive oil

Directions

1. Place a large deep pan over medium heat. Heat in it the oil.
2. Cook in it the shallots for 3 min. Stir in the rice, raisins and cinnamon stick.
3. Cook them for 2 min. Stir in the broth and bring them to a gentle boil.
4. Put on the lid and let the risotto cook for 36 min until it becomes creamy.
5. Remove the pan from the heat and put on the lid. Let the risotto rest for 60 min.
6. Garnish it with some cheese then serve it.
7. Enjoy.

Italian
Herbed Risotto

Prep Time: 15 mins
Total Time: 40 mins

Servings per Recipe: 6
Calories	446.1
Fat	1.2g
Cholesterol	0.3mg
Sodium	779.8mg
Carbohydrates	97.4g
Protein	9.1g

Ingredients

3 1/2 C. Arborio rice
3/4 C. snipped dried tomatoes, chopped
8 tsp chicken bouillon granules
2 tsp dried oregano
1 tsp garlic powder

1 tsp dried rosemary
1 tsp dried basil leaves
1/2 tsp black pepper

Directions

1. Get a small bowl: Stir in it the bouillon granules with seasonings.
2. Spoon the spice mix into 4 (1/2 pint) airtight jars. Top them with the dried tomatoes, and rice.
3. Place them in a cupboard until ready to prepare.
4. Place a large saucepan over medium heat. Heat in it 3 C. of water until it starts boiling.
5. Pour in it one rice jar with a pinch of salt then stir it well. Cook them until they start boiling.
6. Lower the heat and put on the lid. Cook the risotto for 20 to 22 min until the rice is done.
7. Turn off the heat and let it rest for 6 min. Add the cheese then serve it warm.
8. Enjoy.

AMISH
Barley Risotto

Prep Time: 5 mins
Total Time: 30 mins

Servings per Recipe: 2
Calories	552.8
Fat	14.8g
Cholesterol	0.0mg
Sodium	13.6mg
Carbohydrates	93.9g
Protein	14.3g

Ingredients

2 tbsp olive oil
1 onion, chopped
7 oz. pearl barley
2 pints vegetable stock
5 oz. peas

3 1/2 oz. fat-free cream cheese with chives
1 bunch chives, snipped

Directions

1. Place a deep large skillet over medium heat. Heat in it the oil.
2. Cook in it the onion for 3 min. Add the barley and cook them for 2 min.
3. Stir in 1/3 of the stock and lower the heat.
4. Let it cook for 16 min while stirring often and adding more stock when needed.
5. Stir in the peas and cook them for 5 min. Remove the skillet from the heat and let it sit for 3 min.
6. Add the chives with cream cheese, a pinch of salt and pepper. Serve your risotto warm.
7. Enjoy.

South of the Border
Risotto

Prep Time: 10 mins
Total Time: 32 mins

Servings per Recipe: 4

Calories	458.2
Fat	19.0g
Cholesterol	53.1mg
Sodium	837.2mg
Carbohydrates	55.4g
Protein	17.2g

Ingredients

1 tbsp unsalted butter
2 garlic cloves, pressed
1/4 tsp ground cumin
1 C. medium-grain white rice
29 oz. chicken broth
10 oz. frozen corn

1/4 C. whipping cream
1 C. Monterey jack pepper cheese
cilantro, chopped

Directions

1. Place a large saucepan over medium heat. Heat in it the butter. Cook in it the cumin with garlic for 1 min.
2. Stir in the rice with broth, and corn. Cook them until they start boiling while stirring.
3. Lower the heat and let them cook until they become creamy and thick for about 20 to 22 min.
4. Stir in the cream cheese and cook them for 1 min. Adjust the seasoning of your risotto then serve it warm.
5. Enjoy.

NEW MEXICAN
Mesa Risotto

🥄 Prep Time: 15 mins

🕐 Total Time: 45 mins

Servings per Recipe: 4

Calories	369.2
Fat	9.8g
Cholesterol	18.8mg
Sodium	742.4mg
Carbohydrates	60.8g
Protein	11.8g

Ingredients

1 1/4 C. water
2 (14 1/2 oz.) cans vegetable broth
1/2 tsp salt
2 tsp olive oil
1 C. uncooked Arborio rice
1 tsp ground cumin
1 tsp ground coriander
4 garlic cloves, minced
1 C. sliced green onion
3/4 C. shredded Monterey Jack cheese
1/4-1/2 tsp hot sauce
2 C. frozen whole kernel corn, defrosted
1/2 C. chopped cilantro
2/3 C. chopped roasted red pepper
additional salt and pepper

Directions

1. Place a large saucepan over medium heat. Heat in it the broth with water and a pinch of salt until they start boiling.

2. Place a large deep pan over medium heat. Heat in it the oil. Cook in it the cumin with garlic and rice for 1 to 2 min.

3. Add 1/2 C. of broth and let them cook for 3 min while stirring.

4. Repeat the process with the remaining broth until all over is absorbed and the risotto is creamy.

5. Add the onions, cheese, hot sauce, corn, cilantro and red peppers. Heat them for 4 min.

6. Adjust the seasoning of your risotto then serve it warm.

7. Enjoy.

Risotto
Roots

Prep Time: 15 mins
Total Time: 55 mins

Servings per Recipe: 4

Calories	611.5
Fat	22.0g
Cholesterol	36.0mg
Sodium	888.8mg
Carbohydrates	86.4g
Protein	14.6g

Ingredients

4 tbsp unsalted butter
2 tbsp olive oil
1 medium leek, rinsed well, dried, diced, white part only
4 C. of boiling chicken broth
2 C. Italian short-grain rice
1 small carrot, pared and diced
1 small turnip, pared and diced

1 small celery rib, diced
salt & ground black pepper
1/4 C. grated parmesan cheese
1/4 C. diced canned Italian plum tomato
1 garlic clove, minced

Directions

1. Place a large deep pan over low heat. Heat in it 2 tbsp of butter.
2. Cook in it the leeks for 9 min. Stir in the rice and cook them for 4 min while stirring.
3. Stir enough broth to cover the rice by 1/4 inch. Bring it to a simmer and let it cook for 6 min while stirring.
4. Stir in the remaining broth and bring it to another simmer. Cook it for 10 to 12 min.
5. Add the celery with turnips, carrots, a pinch of salt and pepper. Cook it for an extra 10 to 12 min until it becomes creamy.
6. Once the time is up, turn off the heat and add the rest of the butter with cheese, tomatoes, and garlic.
7. Serve your risotto immediately.
8. Enjoy.

CALIFORNIA
Risotto

Prep Time: 1 hr
Total Time: 1 hr

Servings per Recipe: 4
Calories	400.2
Fat	10.7g
Cholesterol	0.0mg
Sodium	367.5mg
Carbohydrates	68.8g
Protein	6.5g

Ingredients

6 C. vegetable broth
1 C. dried shiitake mushroom
3 tbsp olive oil
1 C. chopped shallot
3 C. sliced cremini mushrooms
1/4 C. chopped sun-dried tomato
2 garlic cloves, minced
1 tbsp minced thyme
2 tsp minced rosemary

1/2 tsp ground allspice
1/2 tsp salt
fresh ground black pepper
1 1/2 C. Arborio rice
black truffle oil

Directions

1. Place a saucepan over medium heat. Heat in it the broth until it starts boiling.
2. Stir in the shiitake mushrooms and cook them for 2 to 3 min. Drain it, chop it and place it aside.
3. Put on the lid to cover the broth and place it aside.
4. Place a large saucepan over medium heat. Heat in it the oil.
5. Cook in it shallots for 6 min. Stir in the cremini mushroom with dried tomatoes. Cook them for 6 min.
6. Stir in the garlic, shiitakes, herbs, spices, and salt. Cook them for 4 min.
7. Stir in the rice and cook them for 3 min.
8. Stir in 1 C. of broth and cook them for 7 min until it is absorbed.
9. Repeat the process with the remaining broth while stirring often until the risotto becomes creamy.
10. Stir in some truffle oil then serve your risotto warm.
11. Enjoy.

Butternut
Bacon Risotto

Prep Time: 15 mins
Total Time: 1 hr 5 mins

Servings per Recipe: 6
Calories	417.1
Fat	12.2g
Cholesterol	4.0mg
Sodium	945.6mg
Carbohydrates	72.6g
Protein	7.8g

Ingredients

3 1/2 lb. butternut pumpkin, peeled, chopped
1/4 C. olive oil
4 slices turkey bacon, rind removed, chopped
1 brown onion, chopped
2 garlic cloves, crushed

1 1/2 C. Arborio rice
1 1/2 tbsp instant chicken bouillon granules
5 C. boiling water
5 oz. Baby Spinach
1 C. shredded cheese

Directions

1. Before you do anything, preheat the oven to 500 F.
2. Coat a baking dish with 1 1/2 tbsp of oil. Add the pumpkin with a pinch of salt and pepper.
3. Toss them to coat and spread it in an even layer. Place the pan in the oven and let it cook for 22 to 26 min.
4. Place a pot over medium heat. Heat in it the rest of the oil. Cook in it the onion with bacon for 5 min.
5. Stir in the rice with garlic. Cook them for 3 min. Stir in the water with stock powder.
6. Lower the heat and put on the lid. Let them cook for 16 min while stirring often.
7. Remove the cover and let it cook for 11 min.
8. Turn off the heat and add the spinach with pumpkin, 3/4 of the cheese, a pinch of salt and pepper.
9. Adjust the seasoning of your risotto then serve it warm.
10. Enjoy.

RISOTTO
Hot Pot

Prep Time: 15 mins
Total Time: 35 mins

Servings per Recipe: 4
Calories	338.1
Fat	9.9g
Cholesterol	12.5mg
Sodium	1228.5mg
Carbohydrates	44.3g
Protein	18.4g

Ingredients

1 tbsp olive oil
2 C. chopped onions
2 tsp grated lemon rind
3/4 C. Arborio rice
3 (14 oz.) can chicken broth

1 lb. asparagus, chopped
2 C. fresh spinach, chopped
1/4 tsp ground allspice
2 oz. grated parmesan cheese

Directions

1. Place a pot over medium heat. Heat in it the oil. Cook in it the onion for 3 min.
2. Stir in the lemon rind. Let them cook for 1 min. Stir in the rice and cook them for 2 min.
3. Add the chicken broth and cook them until they start boiling. Put on the lid and let it cook for 12 min.
4. Add the asparagus, spinach, allspice. Let them cook for an extra 3 min.
5. Garnish your risotto soup with cheese then serve it hot.
6. Enjoy.

Tuscan
Risotto

Prep Time: 10 mins
Total Time: 50 mins

Servings per Recipe: 4

Calories	288.7
Fat	10.6 g
Cholesterol	18.8 mg
Sodium	139.8 mg
Carbohydrates	41.7 g
Protein	6.6 g

Ingredients

1 oz. butter
1 tbsp olive oil
3 shallots, chopped
6 oz. Arborio rice
1 tbsp tomato puree

14 oz. cans chopped tomatoes
2 1/2 C. light vegetable stock
1 oz. parmesan cheese, grated
3 tbsp basil, chopped

Directions

1. Before you do anything, preheat the oven to 356 F.
2. Place a large skillet over medium heat. Heat in it the oil with butter.
3. Cook in it the shallots for 9 min. Stir in the rice and cook them for 2 min.
4. Stir in the tomatoes with tomato puree with a ladle of stock. Bring them to a gentle boil.
5. Stir in the remaining broth with a pinch of salt and pepper.
6. Pour the mixture into a baking dish. Cook it in the oven for 12 min.
7. Stir it and bake for an extra 8 to 12 min. Add the cheese with basil.
8. Adjust the seasoning of your risotto then serve it warm.
9. Enjoy.

RICE COOKER
Risotto

🍳 Prep Time: 5 mins
🕐 Total Time: 20 mins

Servings per Recipe: 4

Calories	423.1
Fat	9.9g
Cholesterol	78.3mg
Sodium	817.4mg
Carbohydrates	44.4g
Protein	37.8g

Ingredients

1 tbsp extra virgin olive oil
pepper
salt
1 lb. skinless chicken breast, chopped
4 C. spinach washed and dried

3 C. chicken broth
1/4 C. grated parmesan cheese
1 C. Arborio medium grain rice
1 lb. mushroom, crimini, sautéed

Directions

1. Get a rice cooker: Combine in it the rice with spinach, and broth. Turn it on and let it cook.
2. Place a large skillet over medium heat. Heat in it the oil.
3. Cook in it the chicken for 6 min. Drain it and place it aside.
4. Once the time the cooker is done, press the keep warm button.
5. Add to it the cheese with chicken and mushroom. Put on the lid and let it sit for 6 min.
6. Adjust the seasoning of your risotto then serve it warm.
7. Enjoy

Autumn
Sunset Risotto

Prep Time: 15 mins
Total Time: 45 mins

Servings per Recipe: 3
Calories   307.3
Fat   17.0g
Cholesterol   28.3mg
Sodium   69.9mg
Carbohydrates   32.4g
Protein   7.3g

Ingredients

1/4 C. peanuts
1/2 C. pumpkin, diced
1/2 C. cooked chicken, diced
1/2 C. chopped onion
2 tsp olive oil
1/2 C. long grain white rice
1/2 C. chicken stock

1/4 C. double cream
1/4 C. chopped fresh basil
1/2 tsp mixed spice
salt and pepper

Directions

1. Place a large skillet over medium heat. Heat in it the oil.
2. Cook in it the peanuts with pumpkin for 2 to 3 min. Drain them and place them aside.
3. Stir in the rice and cook them for 2 min. Stir in the onion with chicken, and seasonings.
4. Cook them for 3 min. Stir in the stock and cook them until they start boiling.
5. Put on the lid and let the risotto cook for 14 min while stirring often.
6. Stir in 1/4 C. of double cream. Cook them for 1 to 2 min. Turn off the heat and let the risotto cook for 6 min.
7. Stir in the pumpkin and peanuts mix with basil, a pinch of salt and pepper.
8. Serve your risotto warm.
9. Enjoy.

WEEKEND
Risotto Casserole

Prep Time: 15 mins
Total Time: 45 mins

Servings per Recipe: 4
Calories	678.0
Fat	27.3g
Cholesterol	22.0mg
Sodium	408.8mg
Carbohydrates	88.2g
Protein	20.6g

Ingredients

1/4 C. extra virgin olive oil
1 large shallots, chopped
2 garlic cloves, chopped
2 C. Arborio rice
salt and pepper
32 oz. vegetable broth
1 C. flat leaf parsley, packed

1 C. parmesan cheese, grated
1/4 C. pine nuts
1 lemon, zest, grated
1 lb. asparagus, trimmed and chopped

Directions

1. Before you do anything, preheat the oven to 375 F.
2. Place an ovenproof pot over medium heat. Heat in it 2 tbsp of oil. Cook in it the shallot for 3 min.
3. Stir in the rice with garlic, a pinch of salt and pepper. Cook them for 4 min while stirring.
4. Add the broth with 1 1/4 C. of water. Place the pot in the oven and let it cook for 26 min.
5. Get a blender: Combine in it 2 tbsp of olive oil with parsley, parmesan cheese, lemon peel and pine nuts.
6. Blend them smooth to make the pesto sauce. Add it along with asparagus and rest of the parmesan cheese to the pot.
7. Stir them well and bake it for an extra 6 min. Serve your risotto hot.
8. Enjoy.

Weeknight
Risotto Bowls

Prep Time: 10 mins
Total Time: 1 hr

Servings per Recipe: 4
Calories	625.2
Fat	13.0g
Cholesterol	14.5mg
Sodium	596.1mg
Carbohydrates	104.8g
Protein	20.0g

Ingredients

2 tbsp olive oil
3 chicken breast fillets, quartered
2 leeks, sliced
1 tbsp lemon zest
2 C. Arborio rice
5 C. chicken stock
1 1/2 C. frozen peas

2 tbsp lemon juice
1/4 C. parmesan cheese, grated
2 tbsp chopped mint

Directions

1. Before you do anything, preheat the oven to 400 F.
2. Place a large skillet over medium heat. Heat in it the oil.
3. Brown in it the chicken fillets for 3 to 4 min on each side. Drain them and place them aside.
4. Cook the leeks in the same skillet for 4 min. Transfer them to a baking dish.
5. Add the rice with stock, a pinch of salt and pepper. Cover it with a piece of foil and bake it for 22 min.
6. Once the time is up, stir in the peas with chicken fillets. Put on the lid and cook them for extra 18 to 20 min.
7. Fold the cheese with mint and lemon juice into the risotto.
8. Adjust its seasoning then serve it warm.
9. Enjoy.

CENTRAL AMERICAN
Risotto

Prep Time: 10 mins
Total Time: 1 hr 10 mins

Servings per Recipe: 4

Calories	470.1
Fat	22.4g
Cholesterol	71.5mg
Sodium	240.0mg
Carbohydrates	41.6g
Protein	25.5g

Ingredients

4 1/2 tbsp olive oil
1/4 lb. uncooked rice
3/4 lb. boneless veal, chopped
3 tomatoes, peeled
1 garlic clove
1 onion, chopped
1 pinch saffron

parsley
salt
pepper
1 C. chicken stock
10 oz. frozen peas, cooked
1/4 lb. mushroom, sliced

Directions

1. Before you do anything, preheat the oven to 325 F.
2. Place a large saucepan over medium heat. Heat in it the oil.
3. Cook in it the rice with meat, tomatoes, garlic, saffron, onion, parsley, a pinch of salt and pepper.
4. Let them cook for 16 min while stirring often. Transfer the mixture to a baking dish and cover it with a piece of oil.
5. Bake it for 36 to 42 min. Serve your risotto casserole warm.
6. Enjoy.

Simple

Homemade Red Curry Paste (Thailand Style)

Prep Time: 10 mins
Total Time: 10 mins

Servings per Recipe: 1
Calories	300.4
Fat	3.5 g
Cholesterol	0 mg
Sodium	2368.8 mg
Carbohydrates	71.1 g
Protein	7.5 g

Ingredients

1/4 C. chopped scallion
1/4 C. chopped fresh cilantro
2 tbsps minced garlic
2 tbsps grated fresh gingerroot
1 tbsp freshly grated lemon rinds
1 tbsp brown sugar
1-2 fresh red chilies or 1 -2 green chili,

minced
3 tbsps fresh lemon juice
1 tbsp ground coriander
1 tsp turmeric
1/2 tsp salt

Directions

1. Add the following your food processor: scallion, cilantro, garlic, ginger root, lemons / lime, brown sugar, chilies, lemon / lime juice, coriander, turmeric, and salt.
2. Process and pulse everything until it becomes a smooth paste.
3. Enjoy.
4. NOTE: To prepare a red curry paste use red chilies for a green curry paste use green chilies.

Printed in Great Britain
by Amazon

81508023R00054